Enter the Rubber Chickens

MINI-LESSONS, ACTIVITIES, COMPETITIONS, AND SONGS THAT MAKE GRAMMAR MEMORABLE

KAREN TISCHHAUSER

D0874388

outskirtspress
DENVER, COLORADO

The opinions expressed in this manuscript are solely the opinions of the author and do not represent the opinions or thoughts of the publisher. The author has represented and warranted full ownership and/or legal right to publish all the materials in this book.

Enter the Rubber Chickens
Mini-lessons, Activities, Competitions, and Songs that Make Grammar Memorable
All Rights Reserved.
Copyright © 2013 Karen Tischhauser
v3.0

Cover Photo © 2013 JupiterImages Corporation. All rights reserved - used with permission.

This book may not be reproduced, transmitted, or stored in whole or in part by any means, including graphic, electronic, or mechanical without the express written consent of the publisher except in the case of brief quotations embodied in critical articles and reviews.

Outskirts Press, Inc.
http://www.outskirtspress.com

ISBN: 978-1-4327-9980-9

Outskirts Press and the "OP" logo are trademarks belonging to Outskirts Press, Inc.

PRINTED IN THE UNITED STATES OF AMERICA

Enter the Rubber Chickens *is dedicated to all teachers of English who are brave enough to let go of the predictable and dry and allow a little chaos and noise. It is dedicated to students who want to laugh and remember. It is dedicated to two young men, Justin Glader and Kerry Frank, who said, "You should write a book!"*

Contents

Acknowledgements

THIS BOOK IS a compilation of those things taught to me by the hundreds of middle school students with whom I have had the pleasure to learn. They taught me to stretch my planning and adjusting. They taught me to think and to do something with my thoughts. These pages are some of what I do because my students taught me well.

Thank you to my students, past and present. By stretching my thinking, you have made me better at what I do. Thank you to my administrators, past and present, for allowing me the freedom to try things in a different way. Thank you to countless colleagues for your encouragement. Thank you to Kim Gordon for trying the rubber chicken lessons, but using rubber pigs.

My family, Tom, Sara, and Megan, have contributed to this book as well. They have endured endless stories about what I do each day. They have been burdened with my questions about whether or not an idea might work or make sense. They provided me with artwork, photography, and an actual chicken coup with which to adorn my classroom. They patiently watched me disappear to the basement to write. And they were proud when I said that I had, in fact, written.

Thank you.

On the day that I decide to insert the first grammar mini-lesson of the year, my rubber chicken makes its first appearance. I visibly hold it, playing with it a bit, so that someone needs to ask, "Why do you have a rubber chicken?"

"For grammar!" I respond, and we begin.

Introduction

I THINK THAT before we can ever truly begin to teach middle school students about grammar and its importance in writing, we need to ask ourselves these questions:

1. What do they need to know?
2. What will they remember?
3. What might cause them to be interested?
4. Why do we need rubber chickens?
5. How will this prepare my students for Common Core Assessments?

If we can answer these questions, then we are ready to work. If we have a good sense of humor, realizing that middle school students are not intrinsically interested in grammar, we may see a bit of success.

I will attempt to answer the above questions, first in the most basic way, then in a bit more depth and with accompanying lesson plans, assignments, and activities one topic at a time.

1. What do they need to know?
   They need to know how to communicate effectively in spoken and written English.
2. What will they remember?
   They will remember almost no names for parts of speech, conventions, or rules. However, they will write using complete

sentences incorporating the parts of speech effectively. They will be able to speak formally and correctly.

3. What might cause them to be interested?

    They will be interested if the subject matter is fun, entertaining, and involves laughter at some point. They will be even more interested if there is a chance that they will be recognized for doing well. I know, this answer sounds a bit romantic and cheesy. It is, however, the absolute truth. I have witnessed it.

4. Why do we need rubber chickens?

    Rubber chickens make the activities funny. Funny things are memorable. Having fun makes learning fun. I use rubber chickens because I have them. You may wish to substitute some other toy or funny item for the rubber chickens as you use the book's activities.

5. How will this prepare my students for Common Core Assessments?

    The mini lessons in this book require students to use facts, rules, and other bits of information as they write actively. Identifying parts of speech is never the goal. Good, concise, clear writing is always the goal. Knowing the "why" of things is the goal.

Rationale

AS A TEACHER of middle school language arts, I begin each year armed and ready with knowledge of good literature, reading strategies, plenty of writing prompts, writing conventions, sure-fire test preparation exercises, and rubber chickens. Yes, rubber chickens. I cannot imagine teaching language arts without at least one rubber chicken.

There is something about a rubber chicken that makes things fun. Rubber chickens look funny. They feel funny. They are funny. They make grammar funny. That is an amazing feat. Any middle school language arts teacher would love to make grammar funny. Any middle school student would enjoy grammar lessons that are funny.

I will bring you into my classroom, my world. We will take a look at practices that, on the surface may seem unusual, but in reality are tried and true grammar lessons. These lessons cover phrases, clauses, punctuation, and sentence structure, and the parts of speech and their appropriate usage.

The following pages will give you usable plans, activities, formative assessments (practice), summative assessments (quizzes and tests), games, and songs. Each of the lessons and activities on these pages has been used successfully in my classroom and in the classrooms of a number of my colleagues. The order in which the lessons appear is not important. Most of the mini lessons can stand alone.

The inclusion of rubber chickens in these mini-lessons has no real basis in grammar instruction theory or research. However, the appearance of the rubber chickens causes even the most reticent 13-year-olds to sit up and wonder. That, I believe, is a good start.

Small children learn through play. Middle school students are no different from small children in this way. The rubber chickens allow them the opportunity to play with parts of speech, sentence construction, word order and placement, and other such topics in a typically dry arena.

Where did this idea begin?

Certain components of grammar elude students each year. Even though the rules and usage of direct objects, indirect objects, and objects of prepositional phrases are introduced in elementary school, many middle school students will claim ignorance of these bits of information. They will claim ignorance each year. It was because of this claim that rubber chickens became a part of my grammar instruction.

I wanted my students to identify the direct object in some sentences while we were working with verbs. In order to know if a verb is transitive or intransitive, a direct object must be found and identified.

I read selected sentences to my class, asking for volunteers to identify the direct objects in these sentences. What followed was a game of guess, hope, and go away. Students guessed wildly at the direct objects. They hoped that they were correct so that the lesson would go away. They were not correct. It did not go away.

Out of desperation, I walked to my desk, opened a drawer filled with toys, funny glasses, and other objects found in many middle school teachers' classrooms. One of these objects was an old rubber chicken. Its reason for being in the desk drawer has escaped my memory. I took the rubber chicken to the front of the classroom and threw it to a young man in a far corner. He caught it. I asked for volunteers to tell me, in a sentence, what just happened.

"You threw the chicken," a few students said.
"Yes!" I answered. "What did I throw?"
"The chicken," they answered.

"So, the chicken received the action," I said. They stared at me.
"That means the chicken is . . . "
"The direct object?" offered one student meekly.
"Yes!" I nearly exploded.

Then began a series of tosses, rolls, hand-offs, badly attempted bounces, all to discover that if the action is received by the chicken, the chicken is the direct object.

The bell rang. I repeated the process with the remainder of my English classes that day. When it came time for a check-up quiz covering direct objects, a few of my students double-checked with me beforehand, asking, "It's like the rubber chicken, right?"

I knew that the rubber chicken helped them remember what countless previous teachers and I could not. I was on to something. The rubber chicken came out to help illustrate parts of speech, phrases, and clauses for the remainder of the year. It worked. I bought more rubber chickens. They became a part of grammar in my classroom.

Before the Mini Lessons

BEFORE SCHOOL BEGINS each year, I write a letter of introduction to my students. (See page 113) It usually includes my family information, hobbies, things I might have recently done, books I have read, and hopes for the coming school year. Of course, the letter changes each year.

During the first week of school, I ask my students to read my letter of introduction. I usually project it on a screen in my classroom and also give a copy to each student. My hope is that they will listen as I read it aloud, and then they will use it as a model for their first assignment in my class. This first assignment, as they are usually able to predict, is a letter of introduction to me. They are given a form, or template, to follow. (See Letter to Mrs. Tisch directions, p. 116) They are asked to promise that they will ask no one for help in this writing. They may read it aloud to someone at home, but no one is to make changes or offer editing advice. I want to see what each student can produce without assistance from any adults.

This assignment serves as a getting-to-know-you activity as well as a starting point for the year's grammar instruction. I have, in this letter, real information to use in planning grammar and writing mini-lessons. Since it makes little or no sense to teach things already mastered, I focus instead on those skills that are lacking. These vary from year to year. Some years seem to beg for help in the area of capitalization. Other years have no need for that, but need work with commas. Actually all years have a strong need for help with commas.

Depending upon the most urgent need, we begin our work in the form of mini-lessons scattered throughout our literature and writing practice. The true assessment of success, of course, is seeing students use what was learned during these mini-lessons in their own writing. Success on a name-that-part-of-speech quiz never convinces me that useful learning has occurred. Solid writing does.

This book gives you some mini-lessons in grammar that have worked well for my students. In almost every mini-lesson you will find basic information, short practice, and an activity or two involving the rubber chickens. Then, true assessment occurs as students produce pieces of writing, whether or not they go through the entire writing process. Constant and continuous writing practice using elements of grammar correctly will, without question, make a habit of good and correct writing.

Commas
(Separators)

AFTER READING THE "Letters to Mrs. Tisch," I often begin my grammar mini lessons with comma rules. The way I have seen it, commas are used by middle school students in two different ways. Some students prefer not to use commas at all. They avoid complexity in their sentences. They avoid the need for commas. Other students seem to have with them a pocket full of comma confetti. As they write they take a handful of this comma confetti from their pockets tossing it into the air above their writing. Wherever the commas fall, they stay. In either case, comma work is needed.

I propose a backward way of approaching the situation. We begin with "The Comma Rules" song. I project or write the words to the song on the board. I ask the students to write the words in their notes. Then we sing! I ask the students who know the song "Frères Jacques" to sing it with me. Once the tune is familiar to the class, we sing the new words. Then we sing them again, and again, and again. Just when it seems we have sung quite enough, we stand up and sing again.

The Commas Rules
To the tune of "Frères Jacques"

There are eight,
There are eight,
Comma rules.
Comma rules.
Series, compound sentence,
Interrupter, date, address,
Direct address,
Introductory elements,
Appositive (Jazz hands).

Then I ask the students to tell me what they know about each of the rules mentioned in the song. They might give me rules, but they are more likely to give examples.

1. series
2. compound sentence
3. interrupter
4. date
5. address
6. direct address
7. introductory elements
8. appositives

As we come up with explanations of and examples of each of the rules, the students can add them to their notes under the song.

Their notes may look a bit like this:

1. series – use a comma to separate items in a series (list). A series consists of three or more items in a row in a sentence. Place a comma after each item in the series except for the last one. *The rubber chicken is blue, green, orange, and white.*

2. compound sentence – use a comma before the coordinate conjunction that joins the independent clauses in a compound sentence. *(Independent clauses can stand alone as complete sentences. Coordinate conjunctions are and, but, or, nor, for, yet, and so.)*
    The rubber chickens sat on the table, and we selected one for our group.

3. interrupter – use a comma to separate words that interrupt or break the flow of a sentence. *(Since it interrupts the flow, an interrupter comes after the sentence has begun.)*
    Rubber chickens, surprisingly, help us remember grammar rules.

4. date – use a comma to separate the day and year in a date. Also use a comma to separate the entire date from the rest of a sentence.
    On September 15, 2011, we first used the rubber chickens.

5. address – use a comma to separate the city and town and the state and country. Also use a comma to separate the entire address from the rest of the sentence.
    We asked our friends to come to 123 Feathered Friends Drive, Chickenville, IL 12345, for the annual grammar celebration.

6. direct address – use a comma to separate the name of the person spoken to from the rest of the sentence.
    Justin, please toss me the rubber chicken.

7. introductory elements – use a comma to separate an introductory word, phrase, or clause from the rest of the sentence. *(Since it is an introductory element, it comes at the very beginning of a sentence.)*
    After playing with the rubber chickens, we recognized direct and indirect objects.
    Finally, we were able to pass the grammar quiz.

8. appositives – use a comma to separate the word or phrase that renames or defines the word that comes immediately before

it. This phrase is only considered an appositive if it adds extra information. *(Appositives are often confused with interrupters. They are both surrounded by commas, but an appositive adds a definition or another name for the word before it. An interrupter does not.)*
Nugget, the orange rubber chicken, waited patiently on the desk.

Two more rules that didn't make it into the song
9. to separate adjectives – use a comma to separate two adjectives of equal value that describe the same noun. To decide whether you might need this comma, replace the comma with the word *and*. If that makes sense, use the comma.
10. to avoid confusion – use a comma whenever a sentence might otherwise be confusing. I rarely mention this rule. It just seems to confuse things rather than avoid confusion. I only mention it if a student needs to use it in his or her writing for the sake of clarity.

Avoid the temptation to just give them this lengthy list. **It is boring.** Do something to make the information gathering in this set of notes interesting. I usually set a timer for about five minutes. Then I ask the students to work with at least one other student to come up with examples for as many of the rules as they can. When the timer goes off, we hear from volunteers. Rewards for those who have something worthwhile to add might be fun. A contest between groups to see who can identify the most rules correctly may work. Applause is always a crowd pleaser.

The following assessment may be used as you see it, or with a few changes. I like to use my currents students' names in all of my assessments. The names listed are names of students in my 2010 – 2011 classes.

Commas: The Assessment

Name _____

Please put commas where needed. If no comma is needed, write correct in the blank. If commas are needed, write the rule in the blank. You may use the comma rule song to help you, but you must sing to yourself. Have fun!

1. _____ Mrs. Tischhauser my English teacher makes the best quizzes ever.
2. _____ Damon Bruno and Mike all love the comma rules song.
3. _____ Chris put commas in the correct places but Charlie told him that he was wrong.
4. _____ Before Molly and Hannah read *Twilight* they had no interest in vampires.
5. _____ On October 7 2010 Roland Smith visited our school.
6. _____ We'll learn comma rules by June I hope.
7. _____ Dalton the first one finished has beat Kristin and Mary.
8. _____ Writing beautifully Matt surprised everyone in the class.
9. _____ On the floor in Mrs. Tischhauser's room we found the most beautiful stone engraved with a picture of a dog.
10. _____ Oh we're finished with the grammar unit.
11. _____ Please Chase give me the recipe for your amazing fudge brownies.
12. _____ Write to Moos and Andriesen 215 Eastern Avenue Barrington Illinois 60010 for information about the comma.

After this mini-lesson, I will assess correct use of commas in all student writing. Grade sheets will reflect points available for the correct use of commas. In other words, from now on, commas count.

Complete Sentences/
Independent Clauses

A TYPICAL PROBLEM in student writing is the inability to recognize complete sentences in writing. Often students consider anything beginning with a capital letter and ending with a period to be a complete sentence. I find it easiest to begin remedying the problem with simple sentences, also known as independent clauses. Then we add modifiers, phrases, and even other sentences. Beginning with the bare essentials of a sentence allows the other parts to become more easily identified. Identification of these other parts is only important so that students can recognize complete sentences in their own writing.

Write the following simple sentences on note cards, one sentence per card.

Rubber chicken flies.
Rubber chicken sits.
Rubber chicken wiggles.
Rubber chicken falls.
Rubber chicken rolls.
Rubber chicken balances. *You get the idea.*

Enter the rubber chickens

Divide the class into as many groups as you have simple sentences. Ask them to work far enough away from other groups so that they maintain some privacy. Let them know that they will be performing these chicken sentences for the class in about three minutes. Hand a member of each group a rubber chicken. Ask the students in each group to use the rubber chicken to act out the simple sentence they have been given. In most cases, their acting will involve additional sentence elements. Now, **each** member of each group is asked to write the group's sentence in their notes, adding the necessary new elements as they act.

Now, set a timer for three minutes. When the timer goes off, ask the students to sit back in their normal seats. Ask for volunteers to perform. As groups perform, ask them to read the newly formed sentences. Write each sentence on a whiteboard, chalkboard, or some other place, so that the other students can see each of the newly created sentences.

Remind all members of the class to write what they see acted out. Each student should have a record of this activity for their own notes, so that when the time comes for an assessment, they will have something to use in preparation.

Once all groups have performed, review the list of sentences with the class. You will have a variety of new sentences.

Perhaps yours will look like this.
The rubber chicken flies across the room from Joe to Blake. (Addition of an adjective and three prepositional phrases)

Our rubber chicken sits in front of me as I write this sentence. (Addition of an adjective, two prepositional phrases, and a dependent clause)

Watch as the rubber chicken rolls between Chris's legs. (New subject and verb, and an adverb and prepositional phrase)

My rubber chicken balances on Emma's shoulder as she walks toward Julie. (Addition of an adjective, prepositional phrase, and dependent clause)

Or

While the rubber chicken flies. (You may want to make a "buzzer" sound. This is not a complete sentence; it is a perfect set-up for a dependent clauses mini lesson and an explanation of fragments.)

The rubber chicken sits. (Not a stellar performance by this group, but "the" **is** an addition.)

All correctly written rubber chicken sentences are left alone. All fragments or otherwise incorrectly written sentences are given the help they need. Then **all** sentences are written in the notes of **all** students as a set of complete sentence examples.

Keep the entire list of created sentences somewhere to use in future situations. If you teach multiple sections of English, you will have a rather lengthy list by the end of the day.

Another Sentence Activity

Create a card for each individual component of each sentence below. Every word and every punctuation mark must be placed alone on a card. Punch a hole at the top of each card, and attach a length of string or yarn so that the card may be worn around a student's neck.

Give each student a card from a specific sentence (I color-coded my cards to tell the sentences apart) and ask them to put themselves in order to make a complete sentence. All cards must be used.

You may want to run this as a race, but I have found success in simply waiting for a sentence to actually emerge.

1. After the rain, puddles formed on the pavement.

2. Inside her purse, Emma carried a cell phone, her house key, and strawberry lip gloss.

3. Jake's locker held his backpack, books, a skateboard, and the remains of last Thursday's lunch.

4. Finding a leprechaun is easy; getting his gold is difficult.

5. Is a tomato a fruit or a vegetable?

6. Exhausted from the day at school, Alex sat on the couch and fell asleep.

7. Don't tell Mrs. Tisch about the enormous spider on her shoulder.

8. Is that a mouse in the corner?

Use the following song to reinforce the basics of complete sentences. Your students will not be able to get it out of their heads.

The Complete Sentence Song

to the tune of "If You're Happy and You Know It"

Every sentence has a subject and a predicate.
Every sentence has a subject and a predicate.
To complete a sentence,
You need to have both.
If one of them is missing,
It's a fragment.

Every sentence has a subject and a predicate.
Every sentence has a subject and a predicate.
Just find out what's been done,
Then who or what did it.
The verb is what is done by the subject.

Every sentence has a subject and a predicate.
Every sentence has a subject and a predicate.
To complete a sentence,
You need to have both.
If one of them is missing,
It's a fragment.

Complete Sentences Assessment

Ask the students to identify the following as complete sentences or not. Ask them to mark the subject and the verb in each complete sentence in some interesting sort of way, decided upon by the class. Avoid the old underline once and underline twice. It is just not fun. It is also difficult to see easily when grading. Try color. Offer pairs of colored pencils for the task. Use blue for subject and red for verb or something of that sort.

1. _____ The rubber chicken is under the table.

2. _____ Our rubber chicken flew across the room and into Adam's lap.

3. _____ Because of the rubber chicken.

4. _____ Before we got the rubber chicken.

5. _____ I felt happy when I held the rubber chicken.

6. _____ Before receiving the rubber chicken, we were confused about sentences.

If the answers written on each blank are worth one point each, and the colored underlining is worth another point, this is a ten point quiz.

After completion of this mini-lesson, I assume that students will use complete sentences in their writing. Grade sheets for writing assignments after this lesson will reflect the use of good complete sentences.

Sentence Combining

Following the study of complete sentences may bring you to work with sentence combining. This will make the students aware of complexity in sentence writing. It may force them to use some interesting combinations of things. It will undoubtedly cause a few issues with run-ons and comma splices, but it will be worth it. The student writing produced after this point will be interesting. It will flow. However, it may have errors at first. This is always the case with newly acquired information.

To begin, place students in groups. Make sure that each group has a rubber chicken. Ask each group to write information about their rubber chicken in complete sentences. You will probably get sentences similar to those written below.

The rubber chicken has an orange head.
It is 13 inches long.
It is sitting on the desk.
It has a yellow body.

Now ask each group to combine the list of sentences they have written to make one complete sentence. It may take a few tries to get this correctly written. Circulate through the groups to check for run-ons, comma splices, and any other issues. After all groups have completed the combining, ask for volunteers to read the sentences created.

For the next eight items, ask the students to work alone. These sentence groupings may be posted on the board, projected on a screen, or given as a worksheet. In any case, each student is asked to combine each sentence grouping into one complete sentence. One of the groupings is preceded by an asterisk; it is challenging.

1. The rubber chickens sit in the box.
   They are waiting for their next activity.
   They are wondering when they will be needed.

2. The pitcher looked up intently.
   The pitcher glanced at first base.
   Then he threw a hanging curve, which the batter knocked out of the stadium.

3. Helen raised her pistol.
   She took careful aim.
   She squeezed off five rapid shots to the center of the target.

4. Fearless Fred dashed into the room.
   He dived at the dastardly robber.
   He missed.
   He went sailing out of the five-story window.

*5. Something is true.
   The world is round.

6. Clarissa believed something.
   Her father was innocent.

7. The princess loved a commoner.
   He was flat broke.

8. All the English students loved their teacher.
   The students were awesome.
   The teacher was charming.

You may wish to collect these combined sentences, or you may simply ask for volunteers to read theirs aloud, commenting on anything necessary.

As a final activity for the day, ask the students to work with partners. Give each pair the following group of sentences. Explain that the combined sentence they write might come from a romance novel. Be ready for giggles. Then give them a deadline. These will be collected by you and displayed somewhere in the classroom.

He knelt.
He put his arms around her.
His sleeves were plunged heedlessly in the water.
His shirt and jacket were soaking wet as he clutched her wordlessly.
He was holding her crazily tight.

He was kissing her desperately.
He was kissing her searchingly.
He was kissing her regretfully.

Hopefully, you will receive sentences similar to the sentence below.

His sleeves were plunged heedlessly into the water as he knelt and put his arms around her, shirt and jacket soaking wet, clutching her wordlessly, holding her crazily tight, and kissing her desperately, searchingly, and regretfully.

Karen Tischhauser

If you feel the need for more sentence work, the following sentence activity may help. It is quite active and requires a bit of preparation. Each of the following sentence parts must be written on a separate card. So, you will have cards containing one word each. You will also have cards containing one punctuation mark each. Once the cards are created and grouped according to the sentence they contain, you are ready to run the activity.

Divide the class into two large groups. Once the groups are formed, give each group a set of cards. Then ask the students to place the cards in the correct order. You may wish to run the activity as a race. The winning team can do the third sentence.

The sentences below have worked well for me.

1. According to the Native Americans, my spirit totem is the dog.

2. She ordered a turkey sandwich with extra mayo and cheese, but no sprouts.

3. After school, she had softball, soccer, and then softball again.

The following sentence parts can be enlarged and made into the above-mentioned cards.

my	According	Native	Americans	,
dog	spirit	is	to	
totem	the	the	.	

. ,	extra	She	mayo
ordered	no	and	a
cheese	sandwich	sprouts	turkey
with	but		

, , .	soccer	softball	softball
again	After	she	school
then	and	had	

Prepositions and Prepositional Phrases

A GOOD FOLLOW-UP to complete sentences is prepositional phrases. It makes sense to identify these phrases in order to see the true core of the complete sentence. By eliminating the prepositional phrases, identifying subjects and verbs is easy, thus recognizing complete sentences.

Ask if anyone knows what a prepositional phrase is. Often the answer is, "What's a preposition?" This question is usually followed by someone remembering aloud that a preposition is where a mouse might be or where a wad of gum might be.

Ask the kids to write the following bits of information in their notes.

A **prepositional phrase** is made of a preposition, its object, and any modifiers of the object.

This begs the question, "What's an object?"

Preposition – a word that shows a relationship between a noun or pronoun and some other word in a sentence.

Object of the preposition – the noun or pronoun following the preposition.

*The following pieces of information seem unrelated, but need to exist here to illustrate what a prepositional phrase is **not**.*

A **clause** is a group of words that contains a subject and a verb.

An **independent clause** expresses a complete thought and can stand alone.

A **dependent clause** does not express a complete thought and cannot stand alone as a sentence.
(Most dependent clauses are introduced by words like although, before, because, so that, when, while, and that.)

Now, ask the following questions aloud, encouraging the students to check their notes for information.

So, is a prepositional phrase a complete sentence?
Is a dependent clause a complete sentence?
Is an independent clause a complete sentence?
Does a prepositional phrase contain a subject and a verb?
Can a prepositional phrase stand alone as a sentence?

The above questions may be given to the students as a formative assessment of the material just discussed. Ask the students to number a half sheet of paper 1 – 5. Ask each of the above five questions aloud. Students may write "yes" or "no" next to each number. Collect the papers. Then you can review the correct responses together. In this way, the students will know how well they did before the papers are handed back to them later.

Prepositions and Prepositional Phrases, Continued

When adding to or embellishing sentences, most students automatically turn to simple adjectives and prepositional phrases. Since they naturally use them, it is good for them to understand what they are. The rubber chickens can help, beginning with prepositions and their phrases.

Enter the Rubber Chickens

For this activity, you will need a piece of classroom furniture, a few willing student volunteers, and a rubber chicken.

As the students enter the room, be obviously present, holding the rubber chicken. If this is not your first rubber chicken grammar mini-lesson, your students will have a good idea of what you are doing.

Begin by asking the question, "Where is the rubber chicken?

Hopefully someone will say, "In your hand."

You respond with, "In. Write it down!"

Place the chicken somewhere else, and ask again. When a response is given, say the preposition in that response.

Repeat this process a number of times, moving the rubber chicken to a new location in each instance. You might put it under someone's chair, on someone's head, beside a book, between two objects. Each time, repeat the preposition from the correct answer given by a student, and ask the students to write it down.

At some point—usually when there are no more good ideas or it gets too loud and unruly—ask the students to tell you the words you said after each answer was given. Write this list on the board. Ask the kids to tell you what these words are. Hopefully, someone will know that they are prepositions. If not, tell them. Ask them to write the following definitions in their notes.

- **Prepositions** are words that show a relationship between a noun or pronoun and some other word in a sentence.
- **A prepositional phrase** is made of a preposition, its object, and any modifiers of the object.
- The **object** of the preposition is the noun or pronoun following the preposition.

Now it is time to begin using the rubber chicken to understand prepositional phrases. Begin simply. Place the rubber chicken somewhere. Ask the students where it is. (*On the floor. Under the table. Between Callie and Kate.*) Keep moving it. Keep asking.

Once this feels easy, add difficulty by tossing the rubber chicken to a student. Ask what happened. (*The rubber chicken flew through the air to Jake.*) Ask the students to identify the prepositional phrases. (*Through the air. To Jake.*) Keep this up. Remind them of the definition of a prepositional phrase.

Now add even more difficulty by asking the students to identify the object of the preposition as well. Continue the process, asking for the prepositional phrase, the preposition, and the object. Sometimes, cause the rubber chicken to be the object by placing something on the rubber chicken or over the rubber chicken.

Add more rubber chickens to the activity. Divide the students into as many groups as there are chickens. Ask them to play with the rubber chickens, recording the prepositional phrases created by this play. Ask them to write these phrases in their notes.

Ask for volunteers to read the phrases they created. Fix any problems, and applaud those that are correct.

Another preposition activity using the rubber chickens

Create large versions of each of the following sets of words on strips of paper.

1. behind the rubber chicken
2. on the rubber chicken
3. down the rubber chicken
4. by the rubber chicken
5. over the rubber chicken
6. in front of the rubber chicken

Place the paper strips around the room so that groups can visit them as they circulate through the activity. Divide the students into groups, giving each group a rubber chicken. Supply each group with paper. Ask each group to write all group member names on the sheet of paper. Have a timer ready, set at one minute.

Ask the students to use each of the displayed strips of words to create complete sentences. The sets of words must be used exactly as they appear. However, the groups will add words to the beginning or end of the sets of words in order to complete the sentences. Encourage them to use names of group members in these sentences. They must write the sentences on their sheets of paper. They will be given one minute at each set of words. Position each group at one of the paper strips to begin. When the timer goes off, they must move clockwise to the next set of words.

Once all groups have completed all six sets of words, it is time to perform. They will use the rubber chickens to act out the sentences as they read what they have written. As a group, they may determine who will read, who will act, and who will control the rubber chicken.

The following chart shows a good list of prepositions and how they show relationship.

Location	Time	Action and Movement
above	at	at
below	on	by
over	by	from
under	before	into
among	from	on
between	since	onto
beside	for	off
in front of	during	out of
behind	to	
next to	until	
with	after	
in the middle of		
on		
in		
at		

To assess the understanding of prepositional phrases, you may want the students to complete the following piece of writing.

Prepositional Poetry

Notice how almost every line of the following poems begins with a preposition. In fact, most lines are just a prepositional phrase. You may wish to create your own as a model.

Escape From Trouble?
Away from the scene,
Down the hall,
Around the nearest corner,
Into a doorway,
To avoid getting caught.
Out in a dash,
Without looking,
Into the principal.

Alone at Night
After the last late show,
In the dark,
Without any companion,
But my dog, who barks,
At the sound,
Of someone,
Near the door.
To my bed, and
Under the covers,
I go.

The Flea's Adventure
Through the thick carpet,
Toward the big warm mass of black fur,
Around the cookie-crumb obstacle,

He trudges forward,
Toward his destination,
Onto the sleeping dog.

Clouds
Across the clear blue sky,
Around the entire planet,
Like big soft cotton balls,
Between the heavens and the earth.
Beyond your reach.

Batter Up
In the baseball field,
During the game,
To the plate,
I walked.
Across from the pitcher,
Near the umpire,
In the batter's box,
Along side the plate,
With my hands,
Around the bat.

Untitled
In the house,
Near 10 o'clock,
Without a sound,
Through the door,
Into the room,
On the bed,
To rest for the night.

Prepositional Poem Grade Sheet

_____ (3) Each line begins with a preposition

_____ (3) Rules of punctuation and capitalization for poetry are
    followed

_____ (3) Has been proofread and edited

_____ (3) Is at least 20 lines long

_____ (3) Reads like a poem

_____ (5) Makes sense

_____ **(20) Total**

A = 18 -- 20
B = 16 -- 17
C = 14 -- 15
D = 12 -- 13
F = 10 – 11
Rewrite = 0 -- 9

Another exercise using prepositional phrases

You may wish to show the students how placing a prepositional phrase incorrectly will cause meaning to change. For this exercise, students may work alone, but I have found it more memorable to have them work with partners or in small groups. Present the following sentences to the students. Give each group a piece of plain paper. Ask them to fold the paper in quarters. Ask them to illustrate each of the sentences exactly as written, one in each of the four sections of the paper.

1. With big teeth, the mouse dashed past the cat.
2. On the board, the students wrote the problems.
3. Under the computer, I watched the ants scurry.
4. With mustard and relish, I ate the hot dog.

Once finished, ask each group to hang their drawings on a wall using magnets or tape. Then, give the class a set amount of time to look at the other groups' drawings. After the time is up, ask a volunteer from each group to retrieve their artwork. Now, ask the groups to rewrite each sentence, correctly placing the prepositional phrases. These do not need illustration, but you may wish to have volunteers read the new sentences aloud.

Punctuating Dialogue

THIS MINI LESSON usually presents itself at the time of our first story-writing assignment. Since stories lend themselves to dialogue, it seems appropriate to clear up any confusion before the need arises.

Begin by looking at any fiction story in a literature anthology. There will, most likely, be a good representation of dialogue to use as an example. Ask the students to point out anything they notice about the dialogue (conversation) in the story.

Hopefully, you will get responses similar to the following.
There are quotation marks.
It tells you who is talking.
It is skinnier than the rest of the writing.

Take a look at each of these things and any other things pointed out by the students. Then ask them to re-tell what they noticed. Now, they are ready to write things in their notes.

Notes
Use quotation marks at the beginning and end of a direct quotation.
direct quotation = exact words said by someone

Use commas to set off explanatory words used with direct quotations.
explanatory words = words that tell who said it

Examples

"I can't fly," said the rubber chicken.

The rubber chicken said, "Don't look at me for answers."

"No matter what," said the rubber chicken, "I will always be your friend."

In a conversation, or dialogue, remember to indent the line **each time the speaker changes**. A new line and a new paragraph signal a change in speaker.

"Who is your new friend?" asked Jake.

"This is Graham, my new rubber chicken," answered Mrs. Tisch.

"What does Graham do?" asked Jake.

"Graham can do lots of things. He can be an object, a subject, the reason for a participial phrase, or simply a part of a complete sentence," answered Mrs. Tisch.

Name _____

Period _____

    The following is meant to be a dialogue between an English teacher and a student. However, it does not look like a dialogue because it is incorrectly organized on the page and incorrectly punctuated. Please rewrite it correctly on the lines below. Make sure to pay attention to **indentation** and **punctuation**.

Good morning, Mrs. Tischhauser said Chris. Good morning, Chris she responded. You are looking lovely today said Chris. Why, thank you said Mrs. Tischhauser, blushing.

_____

_____

_____

_____

_____

_____

_____

_____

_____

_____

_____

_____

Dialogue Quiz answer key

Correct indentation = 4 points
Each of the quotation marks = 1 point
Each correctly placed punctuation mark = 1 point

> "Good morning, Mrs. Tischhauser," said Chris.
> "Good morning, Chris," she responded.
> "You are looking lovely today," said Chris.
> "Why, thank you!" said Mrs. Tischhauser, blushing.

16 points possible

At this point, you may want them to review the rules. I like to use the following rap for this purpose. Before I ask the kids to learn the rap, I show them a YouTube clip of a flight attendant from Southwest Airlines. He raps the safety speech before take-off. He is amazing! Then, I ask the kids to stomp – stomp – clap to get a rhythm going. Often, a few students will begin to sing "We Will Rock You" by Queen. *Sigh*.

Once the rhythm is set, begin the rap. Ask the kids to join in while continuing the rhythm. It will probably get a bit loud. You may wish to warn the teachers next door.

The Dialogue Rap
Dialogue is easy,
If you know how to lay it.
Put some quotes around the talk,
So people can say it.
When people in your story have a conversation.
Remember to surround the talk,
With indentation.

After repeating the rap over and over and over and over . . . ask the students to form groups to perform for the class. Allow them 5 – 10 minutes of practice time. Let them know that they will be performing their version of the rap for the class the following day. I have videotaped these in the past. The kids love seeing them. It really does reinforce the set of rules because the students hear them, write them, re-work them, practice them, perform them, and watch them.

After the performance day, they are ready for an assessment. You may wish to change the names in the following sentences. I used names from my classes at the time. I change the names every time I use the quiz.

Name _____

Period _____

Date _____

Punctuating Quotations Quiz

Read the following sentences and add any missing punctuation. You may need to add quotation marks, commas or end marks. Make sure that it is easy to see whether punctuation is inside or outside the quotation marks.

1. I like tighty whiteys They're so white and beautiful commented Lexi

2. Yeah tests stink said Steven

3. Baby toes are so cute gushed Brittany

4. French fries were in the B line today commented Anne

5. If you could only have Xbox and not anything else in the world what would you do asked Steve

6. No I don't replied Doug

7. I love Steak and Shake exclaimed Shelby

8. Connor exclaimed You have a unibrow

9. I like peanut M&Ms commented Joe

10. If I had a superpower it would be transfiguration Val decided

11. I don't like eating candy retorted James

12. Green hair is really rare said Bridgette

13. Hey Colin said Myles You could look at your sister's diary when you're invisible

15. Henry stated Wii is better because it has better graphics and cooler games

You may prefer this quiz. I used it at another time. Again, you may wish to change the names to incorporate your students.

Name _____

Period _____

Date _____

Punctuating Quotations Quiz

Read the following sentences and add any missing punctuation. You may need to add quotation marks, commas or end marks. Make sure that it is easy to see whether punctuation is inside or outside the quotation marks.

1. For some reason I'm excited about the test commented Maggie

2. Peter decided If I had a superpower I would fly

3. I asked you first replied Nico

4. Julia why are you getting white bread asked Lauren

5. Tyler said I'll ask my parents

6. I think it's weird that he walks around with no shoes commented Jasmine

7. I would have . . . uh . . . heat vision David replied

8. Melissa stated The Constitution Test was easy

9. Aaron proclaimed Wii is better

10. If I could clone myself I'd do fun stuff Jake stated

11. The baby toe is cuter than the big toe they proclaimed

12. If I could I would send the smart one to school explained Melisande and the weird one to stalk you

13. Cloning is wrong Jeff argued

14. Halo is the only good game for Xbox Jon said

15. This quiz stated John is really fun

Adjectives
(Modifiers)

MOST STUDENTS KNOW adjectives. They have heard that adjectives are modifiers of nouns, but it is not often clear to them what a modifier is. I like to explain modifiers as the way to make *modifications* to any word design or creation. Modifications are changes or additions that make the creation better or more perfect. Students recognize color words, texture words, number words, words that tell of size or shape. They may even recall a lesson involving comparative and superlative adjectives. However, the use of the very best, the very right adjective often eludes them. The nuance that shows the difference between blue and cerulean, or a whisper and sotto voce, is simply not important to them. They want to be done, be finished, and turn it in.

My concern with adjectives is not whether a student can identify one in a sentence. My concern is whether or not they can communicate to me the exact *which, what kind of, how many, or how much* they want me to see. We need nuance; we need preciseness. We need good writing.

I write on the board the following questions:

Which?
What kind of?
How many?
How much?

I ask the students to tell me what kinds of words can tell me these things. Hopefully, some brave soul will say, "Adjectives." If that happens, we can continue by writing the list of questions in their notes and add to these the explanation that adjectives help to describe or modify nouns. If that does not happen, and it might not, I bring out the rubber chicken. I refer to it as orange and yellow, or soft and squishy, or ugly and upsetting. Then, I ask for more words to tell about the rubber chicken. I get as many responses as possible. I write them on the board.

Ask your students to write the word "adjectives" in their notes as a title. Ask them to write the four questions under this title. Ask them to write some or all of the examples on the board in a list under that. Tell them to add the fact that adjectives answer these questions about nouns or pronouns. These should serve well as notes for adjectives.

To reinforce the information students have written in their notes, you may wish to have them sing the following song about adjectives. Karaoke versions of the suggested tune are available, and they make performing much more enjoyable.

Adjectives Song
to the tune of "Dynamite" by Taio Cruz

I came to say what -- kind -- of.
It might be big or small or me - di - um.
It might be old or young or in be - tween.
It might be red, or blue, or bur – gun - dy.
I came to say which one.
I came to say how many.

I use my adjectives to modify.
Which? What kind of? Or how many?
I use my adjectives to modify.
Which? What kind of? Or how many?
Cause we want color words,
We want number words,
We want modifiers,
For all kinds of words.
We use comparative.
We use superlative,
We want modifiers,
For all kinds of words.

Repeat

Enter the rubber chickens.

Divide the students into groups. Ask each group to describe, with as many usable words (not phrases) as they can, their specific rubber chickens. Set a timer for 2 minutes. When the timer goes off, ask each group to read the list created.

Ask the other students to decide whether or not the words on each group's list are, in fact, adjectives. Use *which, what kind of, how many,* and *how much* to make the decision.

As a quick assessment of this lesson, ask the kids to fill out an exit slip before they leave. On it, they need to write the four questions answered by adjectives.

Adjectives assessment

Ask the students to number a piece of paper 1 – 5. Project the following sentences on a screen or give the students the following quiz. On their paper, they should write only the answers.

Please identify and write the adjectives from each sentence. Use your notes to help you.

1. Giblet is red and yellow.
2. My rubber chicken is prettier than the others.
3. Purdue likes active games.
4. There are six rubber chickens in the bucket.
5. Tyson, the blue and green rubber chicken, is behind the book.

There are 10 adjectives in the above sentences. The answers are listed below.

1. red, yellow
2. rubber, prettier
3. active
4. six, rubber
5. blue, green, rubber

From this point forward, use of good adjectives will be considered a part of good writing.

Participles and Participial Phrases

HAVE THE FOLLOWING definitions available on the board, projected on a screen, or otherwise visually available to all students.

A **participial phrase** is made of a participle plus its modifiers and complements. The entire phrase modifies a noun, so the entire phrase may behave as an adjective.

Participle – a verb that acts as an adjective.

A few reminders will be in order, perhaps in the form of questions from you to your class.

What is a verb?
What is an adjective?
Does anyone know present participle form or past participle form of verbs?

You may want to list or say a number of verbs in past or present participle form. It is easier to begin with regular verbs so that the *–ed* or *–ing* endings are obvious.

Enter the rubber chicken.

Show the rubber chicken "doing" a number of things. *(Verbs)*

The rubber chicken wobbled.
The rubber chicken bounced.
The rubber chicken flew.
The rubber chicken is flying.
This rubber chicken is flopping.

Ask students to tell, in sentence form, what the rubber chicken is doing. Encourage shouting out. Encourage engagement. Shout with them. It makes the activity more fun.

Now ask the kids to switch to thinking in participles.

The wobbling rubber chicken made its way across the table.
The bouncing rubber chicken was caught by Maddy.
The escaped rubber chicken plunged to the ground.

Remind the students that the *–ed* or *–ing* verbs now behave as adjectives. Ask for nods of understanding.

Participle Activity

I print each of the following phrases separately on strips of paper. I hang them around the classroom, placing a rubber chicken beneath each phrase. Since there are six phrases, I divide the students into six groups. Each group begins at one phrase and moves clockwise around the room to all six phrases at the sound of a timer.

At each phrase/chicken station, the groups are asked to correctly write the phrase into a sentence with the understanding that the group will read the sentence and act it out for the class when the stations are completed. Remind students that these words are intended for use as participial phrases. None of these are complete sentences as written.

1. the hiding rubber chicken
2. the amused rubber chicken
3. the amusing rubber chicken
4. the frightened rubber chicken
5. the saddened rubber chicken
6. the standing rubber chicken

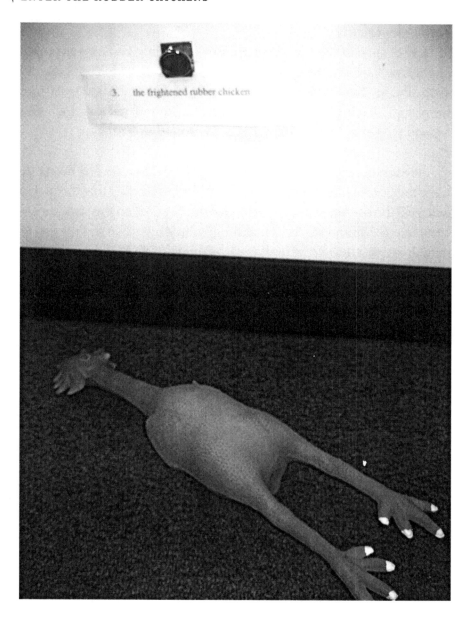

Once the stations have been visited by all groups, the performing begins. Each group will read their constructed sentences while acting them out for the class. Keep track of well-constructed sentences. Also, make a note of those sentences that did not use the given phrases as participial phrases. With the help of the class, fix these issues.

Participial Phrases Activity

Follow the same pattern as before. Hang each of the following participial phrases around the room with a chicken placed beneath each phrase. Ask the groups to use each phrase as intended, as a participial phrase. Remind them that the phrase must stay intact. There can be no words inserted into the phrase. Words can only be added before or after the phrase. None of the given phrases serve as complete sentences on their own. They will be best used as introductory elements to begin sentences.

7. hiding behind the rubber chicken
8. amused by the rubber chicken
9. holding down the rubber chicken
10. saddened by the rubber chicken
11. standing over the rubber chicken

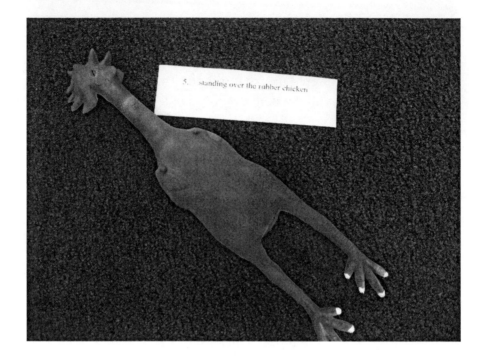

Example: intrigued by the rubber chickens
Sentence: Intrigued by the rubber chickens, other students entered the classroom to ask questions.

The groups can, again, act out their sentences, using the rubber chickens in their performances. Any incorrectly crafted sentences must receive "the buzzer" or some other method of letting the group know it has made a mistake.

Ask each group to give you their completed sentences. You may use these sentences to create a summative assessment for participles and participial phrases.

Clear up confusion about past and present participles used as adjectives and those used as verbs. In the verb form, a past or present participle needs a helping verb. However, in both forms, *most* present participles have an –ing ending, and past participles have an –ed ending.

As an assessment following this activity and the activity for prepositional phrases, you may wish to use the following quiz.

Name _____

Period _____

Use the following terms to identify the word groupings below. Write
the corresponding letter in the blank.

A. prepositional phrase   B. participial phrase   C. complete sentence

1. _____ With the rubber chicken
2. _____ Holding the rubber chicken.
3. _____ Above the rubber chicken.
4. _____ To the rubber chicken.
5. _____ In the rubber chicken.
6. _____ For the rubber chicken.
7. _____ Throwing the rubber chicken.
8. _____ Using the rubber chicken.
9. _____ The rubber chicken is in her hand.
10. _____ There are four rubber chickens in this room.

What is one type of word (part of speech) that can never be part of a
prepositional phrase? _____

Verbs

Before working on verbs, ask your students to take this pre-assessment.

Verbs Pre-test

1. T or F A verb is always in the predicate of a sentence.

2. T or F Verbs are always found next to the subject of the sentence.

3. T or F It is possible to have two or more verbs in a sentence.

In the sentence below, the verb is underlined. For numbers 4 – 7, complete the sentence using the new subjects and the appropriate present tense forms of the underlined verb.

Rodney <u>is</u> tired today.

4. Rodney and Esther _____.

5. You _____.

6. This class _____.

7. We _____.

Now try writing one of the above sentences in the past tense. Instead of "today," use "yesterday"

———————————————————————————————.

After the pre-test, write the following sentences on the board. Ask the students to copy them into their notes. Then ask them to find the verbs in the following sentences. Ask the students to mark the verbs in an interesting way.

We have eaten turkey for the past three days.
I love company at the holidays.
They decorate their house for Christmas every year.
Radio stations are playing holiday songs.
It's the most wonderful time of the year.

Verbs are words that show action, condition, or being. They change due to tense or form and are necessary parts of complete sentences.

A good writer uses different verb tenses to show that things happen at different times. If there is no change in time, there is no need to change verb tense.

walk = present tense   walked = past tense
think = present tense   thought = past tense

Every verb has four basic forms, called its principal parts: the present, the present participle, the past, and the past participle. These principle parts are used to make all of the forms and tenses of the verb.

The rubber chicken teaches us about grammar. *present*
The rubber chicken is doing things to help us remember. *present participle*
My rubber chicken fell to the floor. *past*
It has bounced off the corner of the table while flying. *past participle*

The four principle parts of verbs

Present	Present Participle	Past	Past Participle
teach	is teaching	taught	has taught
talk	is talking	talked	has talked
play	is playing	played	has played

What do you notice about the present participle and the past participle?

They both use *is* or *has* and are followed by a verb in its ~ing form or its past tense.

Enter the rubber chickens.

Using one rubber chicken for demonstration purposes, hold the rubber chicken in front of you and drop it. Ask for a volunteer to say in a sentence what just happened. Emphasize the word "happened."

Hopefully a brave individual will offer the following idea, or something close to it.

The chicken **fell**.
The chicken **dropped**.

Offer great amounts of praise to the volunteer. Then ask what type of verb was used. You will, I sincerely hope, hear the following answer. *"Past."*

Now, ask your students to describe it as it happens. Again, drop the chicken. Ask for the sentence.

The chicken **falls.**
The chicken **drops.**

What type of verbs are drops and falls?

"Present!" a very enthusiastic class shouts. Or one lone student raises her hand and offers the word, "Present."

Now, make it complicated. Ask for a volunteer. Ask the class to watch carefully as this volunteer again drops the chicken. Ask for a new and different sentence explaining the process as it happens.

The chicken **is dropping**.
The chicken **is falling**.
or
Kristen **is dropping** the chicken.
Jake's chicken **is falling.**

Ask the class to think back. What happened a minute ago?

The chicken **has fallen**.
The chicken **has dropped**.
or
Jake **has dropped** the chicken.

Record the verbs used in the activity in a list on the board. Ask the kids to identify them as past participle or present participle. They can add these to their notes as examples.

The following exercise is a re-worked piece of information. I have re-placed the original topic with rubber chickens and the original setting with classrooms.

Number a paper from 1 – 10. For each of the following sentences, find the verb (action or condition) and identify it as **past, past participle, present,** or **present participle.** Please write the correct name of the principle part on your paper.

1. For many years, rubber chickens struggled for respect in English classrooms.

2. In many classrooms, certain teachers separated rubber chickens from other learning tools.

3. As time went on, rubber chicken rights activists challenged such segregation in these schools.

4. Traveling throughout these rooms, brave rubber chickens focused attention on fair treatment of rubber chickens as learning tools.

5. The bravery of these rubber chickens has inspired our teacher.

6. Now, she uses rubber chickens in her teaching of grammar.

7. Thanks to the brave rubber chickens and our teacher, many rubber chickens and other rubber animals are benefitting from their new acceptance in classrooms.

8. Since the successful travels of the rubber chickens, many rubber animals have gained respect and new responsibilities in classrooms.

9. Today, all rubber animals know of their classroom possibilities.

10. However, acceptance into other classrooms is continuing.

Answers to above
1. past
2. past
3. past
4. past
5. past participle
6. present
7. present participle
8. past participle
9. present
10. present participle

The principle parts of verbs show changes in time in your writing.

Two rubber chickens finished their work in each of Mrs. Tisch's classes. This feat stands as impressive in most grammar circles. past (finished) to present (stands)

Verbs have three **simple tenses**: the present, the past, and the future.

The bag of rubber chickens **opens**. *present*

This bag **arrived** in room A-6 a month ago. *past*

Soon, my students **will use** the rubber chickens. *future*

Note
In some of the following information about verbs, I suggest a mention-only status. For many students, the progressive and perfect verb forms are simply too much information. Mention the forms, and explain them simply. However, calling them verbs and helping verbs may be enough. The tense of the *helping verb* is the tense of the progressive or perfect form.

There is another form of a verb (mention only) often used by many students in their writing. The **progressive form** of a verb expresses an action or condition in progress. There is a progressive form of each simple tense. Most students know it as a verb with a helping verb.

We **are using** one of the colored rubber chickens. *present progressive*
You **were using** them before. *past progressive*
We **will be using** these rubber chickens with our classes today. *future progressive*

Since the progressive form is a "mention-only" form, there is no activity included.

Number your paper from 1 – 10. Identify each verb as **present, past, future, present progressive, past progressive,** or **future progressive** by writing the correct word after each number.

1. Why was the first rubber chicken used?
2. A bit of internet research tells this story.
3. Some comedians find chickens funny.
4. They use chickens in their comedy routines.
5. Live chickens will escape the comedy clubs.
6. People are looking for a better-behaved funny chicken.
7. They will be having better luck with their comedy.
8. They will keep the new chickens close.
9. Before the rubber chicken, comedians doubted the success of anything as funny as a chicken.
10. They used the rubber chicken successfully.

Note: If written as a paragraph, these sentences need a lot of work. That might be an interesting follow-up activity. Ask the students to write sentences 1 – 10 as a paragraph, changing verb tenses to make the paragraph flow.

Answers to above
1. past progressive
2. present
3. present
4. present
5. future
6. present progressive
7. future progressive
8. future
9. past
10. past

The **present perfect tense** (mention only) places an action or condition in a stretch of time leading up to the present. Again, this tense is commonly known as a verb with a helping verb.

Many people **have used** rubber chickens for fun.
People used rubber chickens at unspecified times before the present. We don't know exactly when it happened. We just know it did.
The **past perfect tense** places a past action or condition before another past action or condition.
After people **had used** rubber chickens, they began to have fun.
The using occurred before having fun.
The **future perfect tense** places a future action or condition before another future action or condition.
We **will have seen** many rubber chickens before the end of the year.
The seeing will occur before the ending.

Forming the perfect tenses

Present perfect = has or have + past participle

I have played.	We have played.
You have played.	You have played.
He, she, it has played.	They have played.

Past perfect = had + past participle

I had played.	We had played.
You had played.	You had played.
He, she, it had played.	They had played.

Future perfect = will + have + past participle

I will have played.	We will have played.
You will have played.	You will have played.
He, she, it will have played.	They will have played.

In any perfect tense, the tense of the helping verb shows the verb's tense.

In most student writing, especially creative pieces, middle school students tend to over-use the perfect tenses. There seems to be a love for the words *have* and *had* before most verbs. I try to discourage them from using this tense when it is not needed.

A good writer uses different verb tenses to show that things happen at different times. If there is no change in time, there is no need to change verb tense.

Write the above statement on a board or bulletin board in your classroom. Remind students of it every time you ask them to write.

To write about the present, you may use present tense, present perfect tense, and present progressive form.

1. Mrs. Tisch **uses** rubber chickens during grammar lessons. Students **play** with the chickens in her class. *present*
2. Mrs. Tisch **has used** rubber chickens for three years. They **are working** well in her lessons. *present perfect*
3. Mrs. Tisch **is continuing** the rubber chicken use. They **are becoming** a part of her teaching practice. *present progressive*

To write about the past, you can use all three past forms. Using these forms correctly will make it easier for your readers to follow the order of your events.

1. In August, a rubber chicken **appeared** in our English class. This chicken **looked** like a real chicken.
   These actions began and were completed in the past.
2. Students **had played** with rubber chickens before seeing them in the classroom. P.E. teachers **had used** them in strange relay races. *These past perfect forms show actions that happened before other actions.*
3. Our English teacher **was trying** to get us to understand prepositions. She **was moving** the chicken into different locations. *The past progressive shows that the actions were in progress in the past.*

The future tenses tell of things that are yet to come. Using the different future forms shows how things are related in time.

1. Maybe you **will use** a rubber chicken someday. You **will play** with it in English class.
    The future tense shows that the actions have not yet occurred.
2. By the time you have finished eighth grade, you **will have used** rubber chickens to learn parts of speech, phrases, and clauses. With luck, you **will have learned** these things so that you might use them in later years.
    The future perfect tense places actions before other future actions.
3. English students **will be using** English grammar more confidently. They **will be growing** in their knowledge of English, thanks to the rubber chickens.
    The future progressive shows that the actions will be continuing in the future.

The following paragraph exercise will let you know if your students recognize changes in tense. If they do, you can move forward in your writing practice. If they have difficulty, more practice may need to occur.

Project or otherwise show the following assessment to your students.

Number your paper from 1 – 10. After each number, write the underlined verb from the paragraph below. Decide upon its tense or form **using your notes**. Write the correct tense next to each verb.

Many people admit to a fear of rubber chickens. Nevertheless, we use (1) these creatures often in class. When we involve the rubber chickens, we have (2) fun. In a typical lesson, the students move (3) the rubber chicken to show different parts of speech being used. In this way, they are acquiring

(4) knowledge of parts of speech and different verb tenses. During our study of prepositional phrases, the rubber chickens make (5) the lesson memorable. Who wouldn't remember a rubber chicken? According to most middle school English students, rubber chickens rock (6)! In the future, we hope (7) that all students will experience (8) some version of rubber chicken grammar. This will help (9) them remember important facts while they have (10) fun.

1. use—present
2. have—present
3. move—present
4. are acquiring—present participle or present progressive
5. make—present
6. rock—present
7. hope—present
8. will experience—future
9. will help—future
10. have—present

Note that above, the assessment was given allowing students to use their notes. I believe that this sort of allowance makes note taking more urgent and palatable to middle school students. If they do, in fact, have their notes with them, they may use them. They may only use their own notes.

Enter the rubber chickens:

As an activity to reinforce what they have learned, divide the class into six groups. Each group is assigned a chicken. Then explain the following rules:

I will say and write on the board the infinitive of a verb. (At this point, you may need to tell the students what an infinitive is. Students who are studying a foreign language will know. Otherwise, refer to page 73.) I will then tell you which form or tense of the verb you must use. Your group must create a complete sentence with the correct form or tense of the chosen verb and your rubber chicken as the subject or object, write it on a slip of paper, and, carrying the rubber chicken, be the first to place it into my hand. The first team to give me a correctly written sentence using the correct verb in its chosen form or tense will receive 3 points. Second place will receive 2 points. Third place will receive 1 point. If the sentences are incorrect, no points will be awarded. If the rubber chicken does not accompany you, no points will be awarded.

As another activity, ask each group to write the following forms or tenses of chosen verbs on a piece of paper. Once written neatly, the paper must be delivered to you. Again, you will write the infinitive of the verb on the board.

Round 1: Present, present participle, past, past participle
Round 2: Present, present progressive, past, past progressive, future, future progressive.
Round 3: Present perfect, past perfect, future perfect

Use the rules above for scoring. You may wish to keep a running score, or you may score only one day's activities at a time.

To reinforce the tenses learned, and to have little fun with verbs, I changed the words to "Bad Romance" by Lady Gaga. Here is the verb song.

Verbs Song
To the tune of "Bad Romance"

Past, present, future tense.
Past/present participle,
Progressive, perfect too,
We're talking verbs, yeah.

Past, present, future tense.
Past/present participle,
Progressive, perfect too,
We're talking verbs, yeah.

If you want present,
You use verbs like jump.
If you want past, it's jumped,
Yeah, you say, "You jumped."
You use the verbs,
Verbs-verbs-verbs,
You use the verbs.

Give me progressive,
We are jumping now.
You were jumping all over the town.
You'll use the verbs,
Verbs-verbs-verbs,
You use the verbs.

You know that I want verbs,
You know that I need verbs,
I want all the forms of verbs

I want to use verbs,
Correctly it seems,
I want the verbs,
Want the verbs, verbs, verbs.
Oh – oh – oh – oh - oh,
I want to use verbs,
I want to sound smart,
Just like you,
I want the verbs, verbs, verbs,

Oh – oh – oh – oh . . .
I want the verbs, verbs, verbs.
Oh – oh – oh – oh . . .
I want the verbs, verbs, verbs.

Past, present, future tense.
Past/present participle,
Progressive, perfect too,
We're talking verbs, yeah.

You want the perfect
You have jumped before.
I had jumped. We had jumped.
She will have jumped too.
I want the verbs
Verbs, Verbs, Verbs
I want the verbs.

You want the present
You want to say jump.
You want the past, you jumped,
Yeah, you say, "You jumped,"
You want the verbs,
Verbs, verbs, verbs,
You want the verbs.

You know that I want verbs,
You know that I need verbs,
I want all the forms of verbs

I want to use verbs,
Correctly it seems,
I want the verbs,
Want the verbs, verbs, verbs.
Oh – oh – oh – oh - oh,
I want to use verbs,
I want to sound smart,
Just like you,
Want the verbs, verbs, verbs.

Oh – oh – oh – oh . . .
I want the verbs, verbs, verbs.
Oh – oh – oh – oh . . .
I want the verbs, verbs, verbs.

Past, present, future tense,
Past/present participle,
Progressive, perfect too,
We're talking verbs, yeah.

You may be able to find a karaoke version of this song. Or you can just sing it without accompaniment.

Action Verbs and Linking Verbs

In order to understand other grammar parts, you need to know the difference between action verbs and linking verbs. Simple comments made by me might be, "If you can do it, it is probably an action verb. If you can't do it, but it is really a verb, it is probably a linking verb." It was once taught to me, at some point during my secondary school years, that if a verb can be replaced with the appropriate form of "to be," and the meaning is not altered, the verb is a linking verb. This is a fun fact worth writing on a board.

For example, "The rubber chicken looks sad," can be rewritten as, "The rubber chicken is sad." No change occurred in actual meaning. It still makes sense. In this sentence, **looks** is used as a linking verb. However, "The rubber chicken looks at me," cannot be rewritten as, "The rubber chicken is at me." This does not make sense. In this case, **looks** is an action verb.

Note: This mini lesson is essential to understanding direct objects, indirect objects, and predicate nouns. You may want to introduce it before you embark upon the complements.

The following list shows common linking verbs.

be	sound	grow	go
look	seem	stay	remain
feel,	appear	keep	resemble
taste	get	turn	run
smell	become	prove	lie

Linking verbs simply connect the subject to the other words in a sentence, typically complements. They link, or connect, or put things together. Many verbs can serve as linking verbs at times and action verbs at other times. For example, "The rubber chicken *appears* lonely," can be re-written as, "The rubber chicken *is* lonely." In this situation, *appears* is a linking verb. However, "The rubber chicken *appeared* to me in a dream," cannot be re-written as "The rubber chicken *was* to me in a dream." In this situation, *appeared* is an action verb. So, a word may not be identifiable as an action verb or a linking verb outside of the context of a sentence.

Nouns

BY THE TIME students reach middle school, they have heard of nouns. They know that a noun names a person, place, thing, or idea. (See Noun Song, p. 90) They have a pretty good idea that there are common nouns and proper nouns. They may even capitalize proper nouns without encouragement! The biggest issue that students have with nouns is using apostrophes correctly in possessives, and avoiding apostrophes in plurals.

As a review of nouns, you may wish to give the students the following information.

Noun – A word used to name a person, place, thing, or idea
> friend, bathroom, chicken, belief

Plural Noun – a word used to name more than one person, place, thing, or idea
> friends, bathrooms, chickens, beliefs

Possessive Noun – a word used to show a person, place, or thing's ownership of another noun
> friend's, bathroom's, chicken's, belief's

Possessive Plural Noun – a word used to name more that one person, place, thing, or idea's ownership of another noun
> friends', bathrooms', chickens', beliefs'

Common Noun – a word that generally names a person, place, thing, or idea

> teacher, school, chicken, learning

Proper Noun – a word that specifically names a person, place, thing, or idea

Mrs. Tisch, Barrington Middle School, Nugget, The American Dream

Nouns may be used as subjects or objects. The placement of the noun in a sentence tells whether the noun is used as a subject or an object.

Lauren sits in the front row.
> *Lauren is the subject.*

I see Lauren.
> *Lauren is the direct object.*

I gave the Lauren the rubber chicken.
> *Lauren is the indirect object.*

The rubber chicken landed on Lauren.
> *Lauren is the object of the preposition.*

Enter the Rubber Chickens

Ask the students to form six groups. Give each group a rubber chicken and a piece of paper, and ask a volunteer in each group to write for the group.

1. Name your rubber chicken.
2. Decide if your rubber chicken is a girl or a boy.
3. Tell us a short, short story about your rubber chicken. In your story, you must refer to the chicken using the following nouns: common, proper, singular, possessive, subject, and object. For bonus points, also use the correct pronoun and possessive pronoun for your chicken.

You will have five minutes to construct your story. You will then have two minutes to rehearse the telling of your story. Then, you will tell your chicken's story to the class. The chicken may act out the story with the help of a group member, if possible.

Performances begin once the two-minute rehearsal time has ended.

After the performances are completed, ask the groups to list the necessary noun components of their stories by listing each noun and the type of noun it might be. This list may be written beneath the story or on the back of the paper. Collect all stories. These may be useful as assessments for nouns. Just type them, underline the nouns, and ask for identification of the nouns -- or type them, leaving blanks where the nouns had gone. Students can fill in the blanks with the correct noun forms.

Complements

Direct and Indirect Objects and Predicate Nouns

Side note: My first rubber chicken was used to illustrate direct objects. This is, quite possibly, where my ideas began.

A **complement** is a word that renames a subject or makes the meaning of a verb more complete. **Predicate nouns, direct objects, and indirect objects** are three types of complements.

1. Giblet is a rubber **chicken**.
   ***Chicken** is a predicate noun because it renames Giblet.*
2. Giblet has helped many grammar **students**.
   ***Students** is a direct object because it tells who receives the action of the verb in the sentence. Students received the help.*
3. Giblet gave **me** help while teaching.
   ***Me**, in this sentence, is an **indirect object**. It tells to or for whom or what the action was given. The help was given to me. Giblet gave it.*

In order to understand the difference between these uses of nouns, divide them in this way: **predicate nouns** typically follow linking verbs; **direct and indirect objects** follow action verbs; **direct objects** directly receive the action; **indirect objects** tell you for or to whom or what the action was performed. The action is not directly received by an indirect object. At this point, I usually mention that these facts might be written in notes. Then I wink. Then I wait.

The real end goal of this mini-lesson is to understand direct and indirect objects and to use the correct noun or pronoun forms when using objects in writing.

Direct and Indirect Objects

Enter the Rubber Chickens

Begin with one rubber chicken. Drop the chicken. Ask for a volunteer to tell the class what you just did.

You dropped the rubber chicken.

Then, perhaps, a conversation similar to the following might occur.

Teacher: What is the verb?
Student: Dropped.
Teacher: What is the subject?
Student: You.
Teacher: What is the direct object?
Student: Uhh.
Teacher: What received the action?
Student: The rubber chicken.
Teacher: So, chicken is the direct object. The chicken received the action.

Now, toss the rubber chicken to a student. Ask the class to state in a sentence what just happened.

You tossed him the rubber chicken.
Teacher: What is the subject?
Student of choice: You.
Teacher: What is the direct object?
Student: (Hopefully) Rubber chicken.
Perhaps a reminder will be necessary. What received the action?
Teacher: What is the indirect object?
Student: (Again hopefully) Him.

Perhaps a reminder will be necessary. For whom or to whom was the action done?

Now, ask the student holding the rubber chicken to continue the pattern. Ask the questions. Probe for answers. Repeat. Repeat again. Repeat again and again. Ask for different actions and different students to be involved.

Divide the students into groups. I like to use six because I have six rubber chickens. Ask each group to perform at least ten different actions involving the group members and the rubber chickens. They may wish to number their papers 1 – 10, skipping a few lines between numbers. Assign one student from each group to write the sentences down, or ask the students to pass the paper around the group so that each student gets at least one chance to write.

Ideally, have a computer available to create a document including each group's best three sentences. Once all groups have contributed to the document, project it for the class to see. If there is no access to a computer, ask the groups to write their three best sentences on a board in class or on large paper in class so that the entire class can see the examples. If there is time during the day's class period, ask the class to identify the subject, direct object, and indirect object in each sentence. It is very likely that objects of prepositions will be incorrectly identified. Remind them that prepositional phrases are not a part of the core of a sentence. Once they are removed, the rest is easy.

Collect all sentences from the groups. Use these sentences and the document created by the class to create quizzes, practice worksheets, and a possible summative assessment for complements. You may have as many as sixty sentences per class period from which to choose.

Transitive or Intransitive Verbs

NOW THAT YOU have touched upon verbs and direct objects, the topic of transitive or intransitive verbs may surface. An easy way to remember whether a verb is transitive or intransitive follows.

Transitive verbs **t**ake direct objects.
Intransitive verbs do not.

Notice the bold letter **t.**

Infinitives and Infinitive Phrases

The **Infinitive** is a form of a verb that begins with the word *to* and acts as a noun, adjective, or adverb.

My rubber chickens are something most students wish *to hold*.
To hold is the infinitive.

An **Infinitive phrase** is this same form of a verb plus any modifiers or complements. This entire phrase may act as a noun, an adjective, or an adverb.

1. It is a common practice in our room *to use rubber chickens*.
   To use is the infinitive. *To use rubber chickens* is the infinitive phrase.
2. My teacher might use rubber chickens *to help us learn*.
   To help is the infinitive. *To help us learn* is the infinitive phrase.
3. The class took time *to name all the rubber chickens*.
   To name is the infinitive. *To name all the rubber chickens* is the infinitive phrase.

Note: It is easy to confuse infinitive phrases with prepositional phrases since *to* can be used as a preposition. If a noun or pronoun follows *"to"* closely, it is a prepositional phrase. If a verb closely follows *"to,"* it is an infinitive.

Enter the rubber chickens.

Divide the class into as many groups as you have rubber chickens. Give each group the following list of infinitive phrases. Ask each group to write complete sentences including the phrases and incorporating their rubber chickens. Allow them to be funny or even silly, while remembering to write correctly. Then, collect the sentences from the groups.

Ask the students who might need an extra challenge to write whether the infinitive phrase is used as a noun, an adjective, or an adverb.

1. to write sentences
2. to be choosy
3. to impress my teacher
4. to entertain the students during class
5. to find out the answers

You may wish to read the completed sentences aloud for comments. You may wish to use the sentences at a later date as an assessment. You may ask the groups to present their work to the rest of the class. You may wish to do a combination of all of these.

Pronouns

PRONOUNS MAY BE used to replace nouns. Like a noun, a pronoun can refer to a person, place, thing, or idea. The noun a pronoun refers to is called its *antecedent*. Since pronouns behave in the same way as nouns, they may be used as subjects or objects in any sentence construction. Unlike proper or common nouns, different forms of pronouns are used for those different functions.

Subject form:

I	she	you
you	it	they
he	we	

Object form:

me	him	us
you	her	you
them	it	them

Since pronouns do what nouns do, they also have possessive forms. However, possessive pronouns do not use apostrophes.

Possessive form:

my	her	their
mine	hers	theirs
your	its	
yours	our	
his	ours	

Note: In a short list in a sentence, such as Alex and I or Alex and me, follow this rule. If you would use *I* alone, use *I* in the list, and if you would use *me* alone, use *me* in the list.

Example: I played with the rubber chicken. *So. . .* Alex and I played with the rubber chicken.   She gave the rubber chicken to me. *So. . .* She gave the rubber chicken to Alex and me.

Enter the Rubber Chickens.

Place the rubber chickens in the front of the classroom, in a row, on the floor. Explain that the following activity is a race for accuracy and for speed.

Have the following prompts ready. You may wish to add more questions in case the contest is going well. Contests tend to be fun, so continuing might be a good idea. You will read these aloud – one at a time – so that the teams can compete.

Which rubber chicken belongs to your group?
What color is the rubber chicken your group has possession of?
What have you done with the rubber chicken?
Where is the rubber chicken?
With whom is the rubber chicken?
To whom did you give the rubber chicken?

The object of this activity is for each group to identify a specific rubber chicken in the line in front of the class. They must write a **complete sentence** using **pronouns**, not common or proper nouns, to answer the question asked by you. Once the sentence is written on a piece of paper, one member of the group must retrieve the correct rubber chicken (if a specific colored chicken is identified) from the line while holding the paper bearing the sentence, and bring both to you. The first paper will be held on top of the pile, and all following papers will be placed beneath it in order.

You will read the sentences aloud. If the sentence written on the top sheet of paper is complete, and it answers the question, its team will receive five points. The second correctly written sentence will give its team three points, and the third correctly written sentence will score one point. Keep score on the board.

All papers will be returned to the teams for the next question. The process continues until you run out of class time or you feel you need to end the activity.

Note: If a sentence has been written with a specific rubber chicken in mind, and that rubber chicken has been taken, the group must rewrite the sentence to refer to an available chicken. This happens in my classroom, because each of my rubber chickens is differently colored.

Interrogative Pronouns

An **interrogative pronoun** is a pronoun used to ask a **question.** It typically has no antecedent because the antecedent is unknown. That is why the question is being asked!   In modern English there are five interrogative pronouns.

what, which, who, whom, whose

Note that all five words may also be used as relative pronouns. A relative pronoun **may** be found in a question; an interrogative pronoun is found **only** in a question.

In addition, these pronouns may take the suffixes **–ever** and **–soever.** Examples (interrogative pronoun in italics):

What did you say?   With *whom* will you walk?
Who said that?   *Whose* book is this?
Which do you prefer?

Note: If your students have difficulty deciding whether to use who or whom, explain that if "he" works, "who" works. If "him" works, "whom" works.

Gerunds

BEGIN THIS LESSON by asking if anyone knows what a gerund is. I do this for entertainment purposes only. I have never had a student guess correctly what a gerund is.

At some point, cut off the guesses, and tell students that a gerund is a verb in its ~ing form (or present participle form) used as a noun.

Teaching is my job.

Teaching, in this sentence, is a gerund. It is actually a verb with an ~ing ending, but its placement and use make it the subject of the sentence. *Teaching* may be replaced with the pronoun *this*. Since it can be replaced with a pronoun, it must be a noun.

Playing is fun.

Playing, in this sentence, is the subject of the sentence – the thing that is fun.

Now, ask the students for examples of ~ing verbs. Make a list of these on the board for everyone to see. You decide how many you wish to include in your list. Ask the students to work with partners or in groups of three to make sentences using as many of these words as possible taking care to use them as gerunds, not verbs. Set a timer. Give them three minutes to write these sentences. When the timer goes off, ask for volunteers to read their sentences. Make the sound of a buzzer if the ~ing word used is not serving as a gerund.

No Rubber Chickens This Time
Gerund-off

While following a clapping rhythm (the same rhythm used for "Concentration"), you must use a gerund to say a simple sentence. For example: **Swimming** is my favorite sport. Swimming is a verb ending in ~ing, but used as a noun, it's a gerund.

Pat-clap-snap-snap

Ask the students to sit in a circle on the floor. Join them. Begin the rhythm. As the rhythm continues, each student, in turn, says a sentence using a gerund as its subject. Students must move out of the circle if they miss their rhythmic turn, if their sentence does not contain a gerund, or if they repeat another student's gerund from the same round. The game moves very quickly.

Adverbs
(Modifiers)

BEGIN BY ASKING the students to write the following information in their notes.

Adverbs answer the following questions:

Where?
When?
How?
How often?

Sometimes adverbs end in ~*ly*. Sometimes they do not.

Quickly and *now* are both adverbs.

Adverbs can be used to modify verbs, adjectives, and other adverbs. Again, the word modify is used. Remind the students that modifications make things better, clearer, and darn near perfect.

If they can remember this information, they will be able to identify adverbs. However, the real goal is to ensure that they use adverbs correctly in writing and in speech.

Well is an adverb. It answers *how* as in, "How are you feeling?" (I am feeling well.)

Good is an adjective. It answers *what kind of* or *which* as in, "What kind of goalie is he?" (He is a good goalie.)

Enter the rubber chickens.

Select one rubber chicken. Throw it across the room. Ask the students *how* the chicken moved. List the adverbs on the board.

Ask the students *where* the chicken moved. List these adverbs on the board.

Ask the students *when* the chicken moved. List these adverbs on the board.

Ask the students to write the example adverbs in their notes under the facts about adverbs.

Remind students that adverbs do not always end in ~ly. Sometimes they do, but not always. Remind them, also, that prepositional phrases can act as adverbs. *Through the air* answers the question, "Where?"

There you go. Done. Adverbs go quickly!

Note -- Sometimes, prepositional phrases are used as adverbs. In these situations, an entire phrase serves as one part of speech. (See Prepositional Phrases, p. 21)

To help imprint the questions answered by adverbs, you may wish to teach the students the following song. Sing along with them. Karaoke versions of the tune are available in a number of places. It makes performing much more fun if you have accompaniment and, possibly, back-up singers.

Adverbs Song
To the tune of "Firework" by Katie Perry

Do you ever feel,
Like you don't know just how,
To make your message clear?
You need a where, when, how.

Do you ever want,
A better way to say,
Exactly what you mean?
Well, adverbs are the way.

Do you ever want,
To make your message clear,
To write exactly how it is,
Or when or where? It's here.

Do you ever feel,
The need to say much more?
You want your reader to,
Understand you for
The words -- you say,
You know -- the way,
Some use -- ~ly,
Some don't,
Who knows why?

Adverbs tell you where, when, or how.
Adverbs tell you where, when, or how.
They are used to modify – y – y,
Some even end in ~ly – y – y.
Really, very,
Especially and positively,
Adverbs help to specify.
But all don't end ~ly.

Repeat

Grammar Camp

NEAR THE END of the school year, during that time when schedules are disrupted and students have checked out of the learning process, I schedule Grammar Camp. Grammar Camp has become a big deal. It represents the culmination of most mini lessons from the entire year in a week filled with grammar competitions.

I am quite fortunate to work in a school filled with staff members who are willing to help me during their planning periods whenever I need judges or scorers. That helps a great deal. For a few of the following activities, two to three extra adult judges make the scoring much easier and the competition more fun.

Some things to realize before embarking upon a Grammar Camp week.

1. It is always longer than a week.
2. It gets loud.
3. It requires movement.
4. It causes competitiveness to surface.
5. It involves a lot of planning.
6. It will be remembered by your students for a long, long time.

To prepare for Grammar Camp, I ask the students to fill out the following form.

My name is _____

Three people in this class with whom I can work well and get things done:

1. _____

2. _____

3. _____

Two people in this class with whom I cannot work well:

1. _____

2. _____

I ask the students to fill these out honestly. I collect them and begin sorting them to make reasonable groups. I tell the students that I will make every effort to place them with at least one of the people with whom they wish to work. I will also make every effort to keep them away from people they have listed in the "cannot work" category.

This task takes time to accomplish, especially with five classes participating.

The next step is choosing names for the camp cabins. For the past five years, I have chosen cabin names based on unusual animals. Cabins in recent years have been called meerkat, sloth, wombat, pangolin, okapi, tapir, and marmoset. I select names of unusual animals from articles or websites. At the end of a class period, well before Grammar Camp will begin, I write the names of unusual animals on the board. Then, we vote. Each student is given a slip of paper on which to write his or her first choice animal. I ask every student in every class to vote. The animals with the six highest scores will be our camp mascots. I print pictures of the selected animals and attach a string to each picture so it may be suspended from the ceiling.

At this point, scheduling begins. Most of the activities in Grammar Camp can be accomplished in less than a class period. A few take a bit longer. I would suggest having all materials ready to use before the camp week begins. I would also suggest that you secure volunteers to help judge the songs and skits well before the week begins. I follow up with reminder emails on the day before and the day of the competitions.

On the day before Grammar Camp begins, I give the following brochure to each of my students. It sets the mood for the week's events. As they read the brochure, they find out the names of the cabin mascots. They will be placed in their cabins as they enter class the following day.

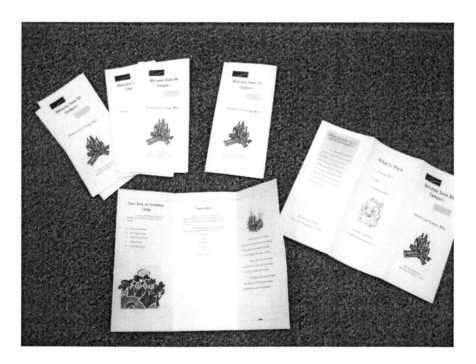

After school that day, I hang the mascot pictures from the ceiling above the six groupings of chairs. These pictures mark our camp cabins, and this will be the seating arrangement for my classes for the next week or more.

Once students are seated in their cabins, they hear the rules of grammar camp. They find out that scoring is done in the following way:

1st place = 7 points
2nd place = 5 points
3rd place = 3 points
4th place = 1 point

Scoring will be displayed on a board in the room and on a clipboard in my possession.

The following activities may be used in any order, with one exception. The Scavenger Hunt (p. 104 - 106) seems to be best placed at the end of Grammar Camp.

Concentration – Grammar Style

The students and teacher sit in a circle on the floor. They start a rhythm by slapping their thighs once, then clapping their hands once, then snapping their fingers one hand at a time. The rhythm (slap – clap – snap – snap) must repeat and repeat and repeat…

Remind them to keep the rhythm moving slowly. If it speeds up, the game will become quite difficult.

The teacher begins the rhythm. The kids join in. Once the rhythm is well established, the teacher calls out a part of speech. Then, in clockwise order from the teacher, each student must give an example of a word that is that specific part of speech during the snaps.

If the student misses the correct time in the rhythm, he is out.
If the student says a word that is not the correct part of speech, she is out.
If the student says nothing, he is out.
If a student repeats a word that was already used in that round, she is out.
If the student correctly states a word that is the correct part of speech, the next student takes her turn, and the next, and the next . . .

At times, the rhythm will simply be lost. Start again wherever things went badly, and continue from there.

Keep the chosen part of speech in use until it is the teacher's turn. Then the teacher can decide whether or not to change the part of speech.

Possible choices for parts of speech:
adjectives
adverbs
nouns
proper nouns
pronouns (will only work when the circle has become small because there are simply not very many)
prepositions
prepositional phrases
conjunctions (will only work when the circle has become small because there are not very many)
interjections (will only work when the circle has become small because, again, there are not very many)

As students are eliminated, the competition will become more exciting. The winning students will score points for their camp cabins for fourth, third, second, and first places.

Grammar Camp Idol

Before you assign the next competition, ask the students to sing with you the following songs. I usually project them on a screen.

The End Mark Song
To the tune of "Hokey Pokey"
You put a period.
You put a question mark.
You put an exclamation point,
At the end of every sentence.
You do the grammar pokey,
And you speak and write correct(ly).
That's how we write about . . . stuff.

The Noun Song
To the tune of "If You're Happy and You Know It"
A noun is a person, place, or thing, **or idea!**
A noun is a person, place, or thing, **or idea!**
A noun can be a subject,
Or an object unless,
A pronoun is the person, place, or thing, **or idea!**
Then, give each student a copy of the following rules.

Welcome to Grammar Camp Idol!

In this competition, you will re-write an existing song **to teach us a grammar rule**.
Then, you will teach it to the class.
You will be judged by a panel of experts.

Here are some recommended songs:

Row, Row, Row Your Boat
Mary Had a Little Lamb
Twinkle, Twinkle, Little Star
Do Your Ears Hang Low?
John Jacob Jingleheimer Schmidt
If You're Happy and You Know It
The Hokey Pokey

The rules.

1. Select a slip of paper from the bucket. On that slip of paper is written the topic of your song. (These topics are up to you, but I usually stick to parts of speech.)
2. Re-write the words to the song to teach the class about the part of speech on your slip of paper. Include what it does, where it goes, and what questions it might answer.
3. Actually write the new song on paper so that it can be sung by members of your cabin.
4. Perhaps, type the finished song.
5. Practice your song.
6. Be ready to perform it for the panel of judges.

On the day of the competition, there will be no time allotted for practice. Judges will arrive, scoring will be explained, and a warm-up song will be performed for the judges. I use one of the songs from page 90 as the warm-up.

The following score sheet is copied so that each judge has a copy for each group performing during the class period. I usually try to fit three per sheet of paper, and then I copy them on both sides of the paper.

Grammar Camp Idol Score Sheet

Period _____

Cabin _____
Names _____
_____
_____
_____
_____

Rate the group on a scale of 1 – 5 for each of the following attributes.

_____ The song taught something to the class.
_____ The "cabin" was prepared.
_____ The presentation of the song was clear.
_____ Words to an existing song were changed.
_____ The Wow! factor.
_____ Total Score

Grammar Grab

In this competition, each cabin will receive points based upon the players' selections of the correct parts of speech from the slips of paper on the floor. You will read sentences or phrases, asking the player from each cabin to identify a given word.

Place slips of paper with the below words on them in the middle of the classroom, face up. Ask the students to assemble by cabin around the room, leaving a good amount of room around the papers. Each cabin will choose a player for each turn. All cabin members should participate. Then, read a sentence, asking for the part of speech of a selected word.

For example: Sophie reached for the ketchup. *reached*

The players must select the slip of paper with "action verb" on it first, handing it to you. If they give it to you first and are correct, they get the point. Play as many rounds as you have time to play. Keep score. 1st, 2nd, 3rd, and 4th place scores get the usual amount of points.

◄ ENTER THE RUBBER CHICKENS

Print the words below to create your slips of paper for the game.

Noun	Noun
Action Verb	Action Verb
Adjective	Adjective
Adverb	Adverb
Preposition	Preposition
Direct Object	Direct Object
Indirect Object	Indirect Object
Linking Verb	Linking Verb

Relay Race

The following competition will take a bit of preparation. You will need to bring into the classroom a variety of product packages. I try to have about 15 – 20 packages. Check them to make sure that you have a representation of each of the parts of speech listed. I have had luck with empty cereal boxes, pasta boxes, tissue boxes, Advil or Tylenol bottles, drink bottles, containers from tea or coffee, soap boxes, shampoo bottles, cookie wrappers, dog treat containers, and cracker boxes.

Scatter the packages around the room so that different cabins have easier access to some and more difficult access to others. I place them on shelves, chalk ledges, tables, the floor, and even hanging from the wall using magnets. Point out each of the packages as you explain the rules so that all students have seen all of the packages. In this way, they might plan ahead.

Have a copy of the sheet below ready for each cabin. You may ask the students to decide upon a recorder to write the information, or you may wish to have the cabin circulate the paper so that each member of the cabin is responsible for writing at some point.

Grammar Camp Relay Race Sheet

Directions: Grammar exists all around us! Just look at advertising! Therefore, the Grammar Camp teams will be participating in a Grammar Relay Race to find examples of our concepts in everyday products. Teams will find examples of these concepts. Teams will use the chart below. # 9 and 10 will be filled in by class consensus. A part of speech not mentioned on the form may be added to the center space on line 9 and 10.

Rules:

Only one member of each cabin may be out of his or her seat at any given time.
Only one part of speech may be obtained from any package.
Only one package may be held by a cabin at any given time.
A package must be returned to its original location before another package may be taken.
Completed forms will be given to the teacher by a member of the cabin. They will be held in the order they are received.
Answers will be read aloud for scoring, the teacher marking any incorrect or missing points.
The cabin with the highest score takes first place. In the case of a tie score, the paper turned in first wins.

Cabin name _____

Cabin members _____

_____

Part of speech	Word or phrase found on product	Where found on item
EX. Proper noun	Starburst	Front of Starburst candy bag
1. Action verb		
2. Gerund		
3. Prepositional phrase		
4. Adverb		
5. Proper noun		

6. Pronoun		
7. Adjective		
8. Possessive noun		
9. _____ (your choice)		
10. _____ (your choice)		

Number correct _____

Add the Correct Punctuation

This is a quick contest. Give each cabin a sheet. Ask them to add the correct punctuation to each sentence following these rules: the paper must move around the cabin clockwise, one person at a time, with every addition of a mark. A different cabin member must write each new mark. Once finished, the cabin must send a representative to hand it to you. You will stack the sheets in the order they were brought to you, numbering them accordingly.

It is a good idea to create a bold and colorful answer key to use before the contest begins. I usually use red or orange ink to make the correct marks on my sheet. You will need to score quickly.

Cabin Name _____

Period _____

1. At 100 we decided to eat we were very hungry after such a long morning of playing with our rubber chickens

2. I ate the chocolate chip walnut and raisin cookie with a huge glass of milk my rubber chicken is blue

3. Since I was going away for the weekend I needed to pack the following items my toothbrush toothpaste pajamas rubber chicken a change of clothes for each day and earplugs because my father snores

4. Practice for the rubber chicken Olympics will begin at 300 and continue until 445.

5. Nugget the youngest rubber chicken has been very quiet lately.

Punctuation Super-hero Skits

For the following competition, you will provide slips of paper with the names of the following punctuation marks: comma, semi-colon, colon, period, exclamation point, question mark, and apostrophe. A representative from each cabin will select a slip of paper from a container. I like to let them go in order of their cabin scores thus far.

Once they select a punctuation mark, they begin their work as a cabin. Allow an entire class period to create and practice. The competition will take place the following day.

The following directions may be given to each cabin or each student. Make sure to read the directions aloud to the class, answering any questions before work time begins.

"Faster than a speeding bullet! More powerful than a locomotive!
Able to leap tall buildings in a single bound!
Look! Up in the sky!
It's a bird!
It's a plane!"
It's . . . Punctuation Boy/Girl

Yes, it's Punctuation Boy/Girl – strange visitor from another planet who came to Earth with powers and abilities far beyond those of mortal men. Punctuation Boy/Girl – who can change the course of run-on sentences in a single bound, and who fights a never-ending battle for truth, justice, clear writing, and the American way!

- Each cabin will select a punctuation mark. It will become a super hero.
- Using the grammar notes available in each cabin, acquaint yourselves with the different **correct** uses of your punctuation mark.

- Create a scripted skit . . . The story line must revolve around your "crime-fighter" finding examples of "evil" (poor writing) and fighting them with correct punctuation. Be sure to include examples to illustrate the correct ways to **use** your punctuation mark, and the **problems** and **misunderstandings** that might occur if punctuation marks are missing or used incorrectly.
- Of course, your super hero needs an appropriate costume, amazing powers, and crime-fighting tools! There must also be a villain (Who, I shudder at the thought, uses bad grammar. *Aaaaaaaah!*). This villain must be ***thwarted***. The presentation should be dramatic, humorous, thrilling, and of course, informative.
- Skits may not exceed 3 minutes in length.

We love Grammar!
We love Grammar Camp!

Punctuation Boy (Girl) Scoring Sheet Cabin_____
                                      Period _____

Please rate the cabin on a scale of 1 – 5 for the following attributes. A score of 1 is poor. A score of 5 is fantastic!

_____ Correct information about punctuation mark; includes multiple uses.

_____ Clear and visible examples illustrating the punctuation rules.

_____ An entertaining and clever story.

_____ Excellent participation by all cabin members.

_____ **Many** outstanding additions (ie. costumes, crime-fighting tools, manageable props, etc.)

_____ A darn-near perfect written script or error-free piece of visual work.

_____ The WOW! factor.

_____ Total

Initial Sentences

Using a person's first, middle, and last initials, create a simple subject, verb, adverb sentence.

K S T

Karen sings tonelessly.

Write the first, middle, and last initials of each person in your cabin. Select four of these sets of initials. Write a sentence using these initials as the first letters of **subject, verb, adverb**. The person whose initials are being used must write that sentence.

The first cabin to complete this task correctly will win.

KST
Kangaroos sweat too.

T J T
Turtles jump tentatively.

Scavenger Hunt

The following is a good culminating activity for Grammar Camp. Before allowing your students to hunt for grammar in your school building, make sure that your administrators approve. Then, warn the other staff members so that everyone knows what is happening. Students will be running amuck in the hallways.

Set very clear ground rules. Warn that any deviation from these rules may result in disqualification and removal from the activity.

1. Cabin members must stay together at all times.
2. Items may be found in the hallways, lunchroom, and media center. No cabins may enter classrooms or offices during the hunt.
3. No answers may be found in this classroom.
4. Cheating is frowned upon.

Set a firm return time for the cabins. Make sure that a member of each cabin has a functioning stopwatch. I ask volunteers to use the stopwatch function on their phones. If they do not have access to stopwatches, they will need to rely on your reminders as you walk the halls to supervise.

Distribute the hunt sheets. Follow the students out of the room. Walk the halls as they hunt, keeping watch on groups. As the time draws to a close, announce the number of minutes left. Head back to the classroom a bit early. As cabins return, number their sheets in the order they return. Cabins have not "returned" unless all members are present. In the event of a score tie, the lower return number will win.

Grammar Camp Scavenger Hunt   Cabin _____

Write what you find **and** where you find it. You must return to class 15 minutes before the end of class time for scoring.

1. Commas in a list
   What? _____
   Where? _____
2. Comma and conjunction to join two independent clauses
   What? _____
   Where? _____
3. Comma in a date
   What? _____
   Where? _____
4. Comma in an address
   What? _____
   Where? _____
5. Commas around an appositive
   What? _____
   Where? _____
6. Capital letters in a book title
   What? _____
   Where? _____
7. Capital letter in a person's title
   What? _____
   Where? _____
8. Capital letter in a person's name (different from #7)
   What? _____
   Where? _____
9. Period at the end of a sentence
   What? _____
   Where? _____

10. Question mark at the end of a sentence
    What? _____
    Where? _____
11. Exclamation point at the end of a sentence
    What? _____
    Where? _____
12. Verb and helping verb(s)
    What? _____
    Where? _____
13. Pronoun as subject
    What? _____
    Where? _____
14. Proper noun as subject
    What? _____
    Where? _____
15. Prepositional phrase ending in a noun
    What? _____
    Where? _____
16. Prepositional phrase ending in a pronoun
    What? _____
    Where? _____
17. Compound subject in complete sentence
    What? _____
    Where? _____
18. Compound verb in a sentence
    What? _____
    Where? _____
19. Use of a possessive in a sentence
    What? _____
    Where? _____
20. Use of a contraction
    What? _____
    Where? _____

Awarding Prizes

At the end of Grammar Camp, as in many organized summer camp programs, prizes are awarded to winning cabins.

Each member of the highest scoring cabin in each of my classes receives a large sticker bearing the motto, "We love grammar! We love Grammar Camp!" Each member of this cabin also receives a tiny rubber chicken. These are wildly popular, but tend to be a bit pricey.

Each member of the second place team in each of my classes receives a large sticker.

All students receive tiny stickers bearing the "We love grammar! We love Grammar Camp!" motto.

Then, we celebrate a successful camp with some version or another of s'mores. About four years ago, I decided to make s'mores using microwave ovens from various other teachers' classrooms. These teachers were kind enough to loan their ovens to me for the day. I proceeded to put the ingredients together, and when heating them in the microwaves, I took out the power of my entire wing. I no longer make s'mores (nor am I allowed to) in the classroom. I have found that granola bars come in s'mores flavor. Now, I either buy an incredibly large number of granola bars for the event or I make s'mores trail mix using mini marshmallows, tiny graham crackers, and chocolate chips.

National Grammar Day

AS A PART of your grammar study, and to have a little fun, you may wish to celebrate National Grammar Day. A few of my students made me aware of this under-celebrated holiday. Their enthusiasm encouraged me to honor the day. I convinced a number of English teachers to participate in the assignment below. Then we displayed some of the work on two rather large bulletin boards in a very public area of the school.

The assignment explanation below gave way to a flurry of activity. There were discussions involving sonnets, love songs, lyrics to existing songs, appropriate wordings for old-fashioned love letters, and of course, the finer points of the selected grammar topics. The class period was not long enough to accommodate everything going on. However, I rather like it that way. The students took with them the beginnings of their writing, perfected their work on their own, and gave me final copies adorned with hearts, lace, pink and red ink, scented paper, and gushy love writing.

The bulletin boards looked as sugary sweet as a Valentine's Day display.

Directions for the proposed assignment are found on the next page.

We love grammar. Who doesn't?

March 4, **National Grammar Day**, is the perfect day to show grammar our *love*.

As a labor of love, and in honor of National Grammar Day, I ask you to select one of the options below. Show your love. Show your deepest feelings. Show grammar that you care.

You may select one of the following parts of speech.

noun   verb   adjective   adverb   preposition
conjunction   interjection

Or you may select one of the following punctuation marks

period   comma   question mark   exclamation mark
quotation marks   apostrophe   dash   semi-colon
colon

Or you may select one of the following phrases or clauses.

prepositional phrase   participial phrase   dependent clause
independent clause

Then, you may select and circle one of the following writing forms with which to show your love.

love letter   poem   lyrics to an existing song

Once you decide, begin to put your thoughts in order. What does this part of speech, punctuation mark, or phrase or clause do? How does it help writers? Why would you be lost without it? What does it help you say? Keep going. You are on a roll.

Then, think about form and style. Does your word choice lend itself to this sort of letter or poem? What would make it more convincing?

Craft. Write. Play with word choices. Cross out. Re-write. Re-think. Write more. Sweat a little. Change a few words. Add a few words. Make some decisions.

Once you are satisfied with your work, read it aloud. Really listen to it. Change some more. The rough draft of this assignment will be completed before you leave class today. The final copy of this piece of writing will be turned in on March 8.

Note: Select poems, lyrics, and letters will be displayed proudly on the bulletin boards at the end of the A wing for all to enjoy.

Happy writing.
The Management

I always complete any assignment given to my students. I give myself an earlier due date, so that the students can see where my expectations truly lie. Here is my love note to the apostrophe.

March 4

Apostrophe, my love,

You make me whole. You put my pieces together when I feel disjointed and separate. You are the glue that keeps me one.

Before I met you, dear Apostrophe, I left pieces unjoined, ideas unmeshed. I was choppy, breathy, and incohesive. Now that I have found you, my world is joined, meshed, and solid. My words flow together in musical legato, breathless, not breathy. Apostrophe, dear Apostrophe, you make me whole. With one tiny curve, you can meld two seemingly separate words into one or cause possession – belonging in its deepest sense.

You're everything to me. I'm indebted to you. I've nearly forgotten a world in which you've not yet existed. We're destined to stay together. We've got to press on joining, blending, and combining. It's meant to be. We're inseparable. I've no doubt, Apostrophe, that you'll make life easier for me.

You're my life, my everything. I've but one request; join with me in love. I would love to be Apostrophe's.

Fondly,
Karen

Afterward

THIS BOOK IS not meant to replace a grammar textbook. It is meant to enhance an already existing program of writing and communicating. It is meant to add life to an otherwise predictable subject area. It is meant to make grammar memorable for students.

I hope that you will find something in these pages to use. I hope that you will have some fun using it. I hope that your students will enjoy it and remember it. I look forward to hearing from you.

Dear Students:

This is my ninth year teaching at BMS Station. My first two years were spent teaching 6th grade, and then I taught 7th grade for three years. Now, I begin my fourth year working in eighth grade. I noticed quite a few familiar last names on my class lists for the coming year. Please understand that I will probably not mention older brothers or sisters to any of you unless you bring it up. I am the youngest of three children, and I found it much more pleasant if teachers did not compare me to my older siblings. So, I will not compare you to yours.

I have worked with middle school students in Woodridge, Cary, and Vernon Hills, Illinois. Then, our family moved to Alpharetta, Georgia, where we lived for five years. After that, we lived in Kelkheim, Germany, and I worked as a permanent substitute teacher in Oberursel, at the Frankfurt International School. Shortly after we moved to the Barrington area, I began teaching here.

I love reading and writing. I read just about everything I can, and I try to write often. Be prepared. You will be asked to read and write often. Just ask anyone who had me last year. My ideas for teaching and for writing come from the books I read, the movies I watch, the thoughts I have while walking my dog, things that people say, and everyday things that happen to me. Our plans will change from day to day. Nothing is set in stone. You will soon notice that our English class may be different than other English classes. The real difference is that I have no idea what I will teach you! Really! I need to meet you, find out what you need, and work from there. Teaching middle school students is something I love to do. I tend to do it best by doing a variety of things. My goal is to surprise you, amaze you, and astound you. At the very least, I hope to get you thinking. I would love to make you aware of your thinking and encourage you to think about your thinking.

This year I will expose you to reading, writing, speaking, and listening. You will probably like some of the things we do, but you may not like everything we do. I invite you to try everything that we do so that you can make an informed decision. I like to think of reading and writing as things you must practice. With practice, reading and writing will become easier and more enjoyable. Some of the practice will be just that – practice that will not turn into anything final. Other things will be perfected and tweaked until they are ready for publication. These will be read, marked, and graded by me. I grade all writing in pencil. I complete every writing assignment that I invite you to complete. Usually, my due date is earlier than yours so that you can see what I expect. You will often be asked to critique my work. Your homework will often include reading, tweaking your writing, and completing anything you were unable to complete in class (*sigh*).

My husband Tom and I have two daughters, Sara and Megan. Sara graduated from the University of Illinois last May with two degrees, one in chemistry and the other in psychology. This year, she is teaching chemistry and organic chemistry Merit discussions at the University of Illinois until she finds out which graduate program she will enter. Megan is beginning her junior year at New York University, in Greenwich Village, in New York City. She is studying vocal performance and musical theater. Over the summer, she taught private voice lessons and dance lessons as well as musical theater camps at the Barrington Performing Artz Center. She also attended classes at Northwestern University.

Our yellow lab, Gwen, will be seven in November. She and I walk together every day before school, and some days after school as well. I give her credit for helping me to create activities and assignments while we walk. She never disrupts my thinking. We rescued her about six-and-a-half years ago. She coexists well with our green and yellow parakeet named Mimi. She comes out of her cage to exercise, but lately, she doesn't often leave her cage. She just sits on top. We have tried to get her to talk, but she's not interested.

When I am not here, I spend time walking Gwen, cooking,

baking, spending time with my husband and daughters, reading, and writing. I spent a few days at Northwestern University over the summer at a writing conference. I am putting the finishing touches on my first book, and have a second book started. I hope to have them published, but I hear that may take a long time. I will keep you posted. I also read about 15 – 20 books over the summer. I absolutely loved *The Land of Painted Caves* by Jean Auel. It is the final book in a series called *The Earth's Children*. I have been waiting for it for about eight years! I like a lot of books, but some books that I found I could not put down were *The Book Thief, Garden Spells, The Thirteenth Tale, The Elegance of the Hedgehog, Fablehaven, The Lost Symbol, Molokai,* and *Unbroken*. There is a stack of books waiting for me on the table next to my favorite chair, and a virtual stack in my Nook.

In June, when I look back on this year, I hope that I will feel good about our time together. I hope that you will accept my invitation to read and write. I hope that your writing and our talking will help me to know you. I hope that we will have attitudes and opinions about things, and that we will be able to say what we mean. I hope to have prepared you for high school without losing sight of this year. I hope that this year will have been a time of growth for you and for me. I hope that I will instill in you a love of learning and the desire to show real pride in your work. I hope that when you look back on what you have done at the end of the year, you will be proud.

Here's to a really good year.

Sincerely,

Karen Tischhauser

Letter to Mrs. Tisch -- Directions

August 2011

Dear Mrs. Tisch:

Paragraph 1 – Tell me about you. What things should I know if I plan to work with you this year? What sets you apart from other students? What interests and abilities do you have? Tell me something I wouldn't know simply by looking at you. Trust me, I know that you are in eighth grade, in my class, and can probably figure out your hair and eye color.

Paragraph 2 – What kind of learner are you? What types of things have worked for you in school in the past? What types of things have not worked for you in the past? What would you say is the best thing you have done in school so far? Tell about the bests and worsts of last year. What books and assignments worked for you? Which ones didn't?

Paragraph 3 -- What are you looking forward to in 8th grade? What do you expect of me as one of your teachers? What do you need from me?

Paragraph 4 – What kinds of books do you like to read? Have you ever read a book without being asked to? Is there a certain book that you felt you couldn't put down? What was it? What helps you to enjoy reading a book?

Paragraph 5 – (Yes, there will be five complete paragraphs.) When you look back on this year, what will you have accomplished? Pretend it is June. You are re-capping the year in English class. How did it go? Explain.

Sincerely/Yours truly/or a closing of your choice,

Your name

*The above letter will be turned in typed in 12 pt. font, double spaced **or** written in your absolute neatest handwriting on one side of the page only. Thank you.*

CPSIA information can be obtained at www.ICGtesting.com
Printed in the USA
LVOW08s0749161013

357154LV00001B/3/P